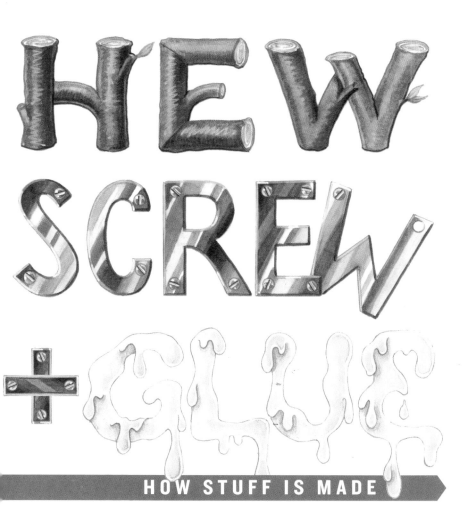

HEW SCREW + GLUE

HOW STUFF IS MADE

JAMES INNES-SMITH   ILLUSTRATED BY HENRIETTA WEBB

ABRAMS IMAGE, NEW YORK

Editor: Tamar Brazis
Designer: Alissa Faden
Production Manager: Jacquie Poirier

Library of Congress Cataloging-in-Publication Data

Innes-Smith, James.
  Hew, screw, and glue : how stuff is made / by James Innes-Smith ; illustrated by
Henrietta Webb.
    p. cm.
  ISBN 978-0-8109-8259-8
  1. Manufactures—Popular works. 2. Materials—Popular works. 3. Curiosities and
wonders—Popular works. I. Webb, Henrietta. II. Title.
  TS146.I55 2009
  670—dc22
2008038455

Printed and bound in China
10 9 8 7 6 5 4 3 2 1

Abrams Image books are available at special discounts when purchased in quantity
for premiums and promotions as well as fundraising or educational use. Special
editions can also be created to specification. For details, contact specialmarkets@
hnabooks.com or the address below.

HNA
harry n. abrams, inc.
a subsidiary of La Martinière Groupe

115 West 18th Street
New York, NY 10011
www.hnabooks.com

To Bobby and Betsy

CONTENTS

Books have come a long way since the Egyptians first began writing on clay tablets and papyrus rolls more than five thousand years ago. A couple of millennia later, the Chinese were making books out of bamboo strips bound together with cord. But it wasn't until the fifteenth century and the invention of the printing press that books as we know them today existed. In 1456, Johann Gutenburg of Germany printed the first ever book, a Latin version of the Bible, on his patented hand-printing press. Each letter was designed to resemble actual handwriting and had to be painstakingly laid by hand. Over the last hundred years, book production has flourished as printing methods have improved. The number of books published each year is now well over one million—that's 167 books for every one million humans. Believe it or not, a book is published somewhere in the world every thirty seconds. So, how did this book that you are holding in your hands come to exist?

First, I researched and wrote the book. I then sent the manuscript to an editor. Having been edited and checked for grammar and punctuation, it was given to a designer, who came up with details such as which font to use, what size the type should be, and how the illustrations would be laid out. Because this particular book contains lots of illustrations, the publisher needed to hire an illustrator, in this case the talented artist Henrietta Webb. Once the layouts were complete and free of errors, they were sent off to the printers, usually in the Far East, where costs are much cheaper.

But you can't print a book without pages, and you can't have pages without paper. About half of the fiber used in paper comes from specially grown trees such as conifer, spruce, and fir. The extra-long cellulose fibers found in these particular trees give

IT'S A FACT...

▸ A book can only officially be called a book if it is more than forty-nine pages long!

▸ A person who loves books is called a bibliophile.

▸ Paper is designed so that ink actually sits on the surface rather than sinking in.

▸ Often referred to as the "intellectuals of the working class," typesetters of old had privileged access to all the great literary works as they positioned each letter of the manuscript by hand.

▸ The Bible is the bestselling book of all time.

▸ The word "book" comes from the Old English word "bok."

paper its strength. Other ingredients include fiber from sawmills, recycled newspaper, vegetable matter, and cloth. Dyes and bleaches give paper its look, while fillers (chalk and clay) and sizings (gum and starch) create absorbency and help to bind everything together.

After the trees have been felled, they are chopped up and placed in large revolving drums that remove the bark. The stripped logs are then crushed between two enormous revolving slabs called *grinders*. The resulting wood chips are poured into huge vats or digesters and boiled in a solution of sodium hydroxide and sodium sulfide until the whole mixture dissolves into a mulchy pulp, which is then filtered. Bleach or coloring is added before the pulp is sent to a paper plant, where it is pounded and squeezed in a process known as *beating*. Starch is added to the mixture to make the paper resistant to water-based ink.

The mulch is pressed between two large rollers that squeeze out the excess water. Steam-heated cylinders evaporate any remaining moisture. The dry paper is then wound onto massive reels and passed between metal rollers known as *calenders* that give the paper either a soft, dull, hard, or shiny finish. The paper is now ready to be cut into book-sized sheets.

When the publisher's layouts arrive at the separator, the pages are photographed. The negative image of each page is laid out in order on a large sheet known as a *flat* or *goldenrod* that holds either thirty-two or sixty-four pages. A print worker known as a *stripper* then checks that all the text has been lined up correctly. A proof of each flat is made by shining an ultraviolet light through the negatives to expose the text images onto light-sensitive paper. The paper and text appear blue, hence the term *blueprint*. If any final changes are to be made, the page or pages in question need to be reprinted and photographed again. When everything is perfect, the

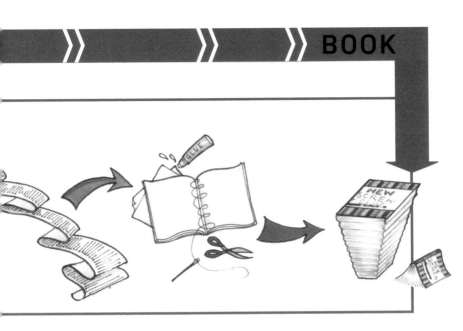

flats are photographed and the negative image is burned onto a sheet of aluminium known as a *plate*.

The plates, which have been treated with special ink-attracting chemicals, are sent off to the printing press. Thirty-two or sixty-four sequenced pages are printed onto each flat, and these are sent to the binders. The flats are then folded along each page to form sections or *signatures* that are sewn or glued together. The cover and spine are glued in place, encasing the finished work in either a soft or hard cover.

Once the book has been printed, it's up to the publisher's sales team to persuade bookstores to stock the title. If bookstore buyers like what they see, they order copies. The marketing and publicity departments then try to drum up attention by sending copies to newspapers, magazines, and TV and radio stations. So whether you read about it in a magazine or just liked the cover, *Hew, Screw, and Glue* has been on quite a journey to get to you!

Ten-pin bowling has been a popular pastime for longer than you might expect. A recent excavation of a child's tomb in Egypt revealed a set of stone pins and a stone ball said to be more than five thousand years old.

The first bowling balls to be manufactured in the United States were originally made of wood such as oak or lignum vitae. At the beginning of the twentieth century, rubber balls took over and were popular up until the 1970s, when the first polyester ball was developed. In the 1980s, the interior of the bowling ball changed dramatically. A reactive urethane exterior coating, or *resin,* was also added. The modern bowling ball may look simple, but underneath that humble exterior is a precision piece of engineering designed to help you achieve strike after strike.

The manufacturing process begins with the revolutionary *core,* which forms the nucleus of the ball. There are more than twenty-four different shapes and densities of core, but essentially what they do is give the ball weight and balance. The shape of the core defines how the ball will roll. Although bowling balls are classified by weight, the real issue is mass, i.e., how the ball will shake and twist as it speeds down the lane. The asymmetrical cores mean that bowling balls don't actually roll, they wobble. Making the ball imbalanced actually gives it power steering, allowing the player to have more control over how the ball hits the pins. A core twists across three axes, so it's important that the positioning is right during production.

Two precision holes are drilled into the core to mark out the principal axis point. A long pin is then inserted into the hole, where it will remain as a marker throughout the rest of the production process. Eventually this pin will show where the finger holes should be drilled. The combination of finger holes and core positioning give the ball hook and accuracy. The core is now centered

IT'S A FACT...

▶ A five-pin bowling ball has no holes but is smaller than the regular tenpin finger ball so that it fits in the palm of the hand.

▶ Regulation ten-pin bowling balls must weigh no more than sixteen pounds and have a diameter of 8.5 inches.

▶ The first bowling balls used in the United States were made of oak.

▶ Over seventy million Americans hit the bowling lanes every year.

▶ Ebonite, one of the world's largest bowling ball manufacturers, produces around five thousand balls per day!

▶ In the 1800s the popular sport of nine-pin bowling was outlawed in certain U.S. states because it was considered to be a form of gambling. A tenth pin was therefore added to avoid prosecution.

inside a spherical mold, which is then filled with resin to form the outer core. Here comes the tricky part. Each ball has to be exactly twenty-seven inches in circumference, but it can weigh between six and sixteen pounds. To achieve different weights without adding to the size, the outer core is made out of a dense material mixed with an extremely light powder. The powder is comprised of tiny glass micro-bubbles full of air. By mixing these two fillers together in different proportions, it is possible to vary the weight without having to change the ball size.

Before the outer core is added, the inner core needs to be positioned and centered within the mold. The resin is then poured into the mold and left to harden. The hardened ball is placed inside another mold ready for the special plastic coating to be added.

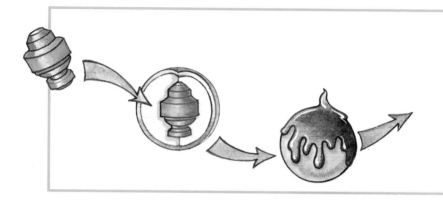

This is made up of two sets of molecules and plasticizers that react violently together to form a viscous glob. As the plasticizers evaporate, they leave microscopic holes in the ball's surface that will then soak up some of the oil on the surface of the bowling lane. This gives the ball extra traction, which allows it to change rotation on its preferred axis and hook the pins from the side. The side area of the lane, known as the pocket, is where most strikes occur.

Our beautifully honed bowling ball now needs to be baked in a hot oven for extra strength. As the plasticizers heat up, they continue to evaporate, making the surface of the ball harder and more porous. The ball is then moved from the oven straight to a refrigerator, where the coating is left to cool. Those pin heads that are still sticking out of the ball mark where the finger holes will go. But before the holes are drilled, that power steering needs to be tested, so the ball is placed on a special machine and spun at high speed to check that it remains on its preferred axis. The ball also needs tread to help it tear across the oily lane at a high velocity and strike the pins with extra power. To achieve a good tread, the

BOWLING BALL

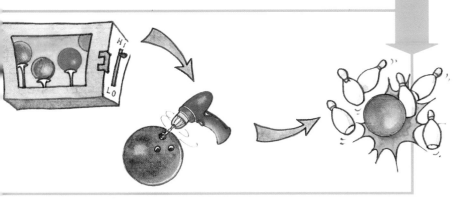

ball needs to be smooth and highly polished. A shaver therefore grinds a tenth of an inch off the circumference of the ball, removing any lingering irregularities. The ball is then covered in polish and buffed to a mirror finish. The final stage of the process is to drill those all-important finger holes. For customized bowling balls, an engineer measures the size of a player's fingers and grip span, and then determines the exact positioning of the holes using the pin marks as a guide. With the help of a precision lathe, he drills the three holes.

Before balls are sold, they must first be tested on an actual lane, where a video tracking device records the entire journey of the ball, comparing and analyzing the results against how the ball would react under ideal circumstances. If everything is in order, our ball is ready to strike out on one of America's six thousand bowling alleys.

So now that you know how a bowling ball is made, it's time to start practicing your game. And remember, just as in life, bowling is full of strikes and gutter balls, so don't give up!

When ancient man discovered fire, he not only found a means
of cooking and keeping warm but also a way to see in the dark.
Just because the sun went down didn't mean life had to come to
a standstill! History shows that candles were one of the earliest
forms of portable lighting, and evidence of their existence has
been discovered all over the world. The earliest candles were
made from branches dipped in animal fat. Bowl-shaped candles
made of sheep fat have been found on the island of Crete and
date back to 3000 BCE. The Sung Dynasty in China (960–1279
CE) used candles as clocks because of the evenness with which
they burned. A form of candle-clock was still used in coal mining
right up until the early twentieth century.

The materials may have changed over the years, but the process of candle making remains remarkably unchanged. Before the
mid-nineteenth century, candles tended to be made of *tallow*, a
by-product of beef fat. But they gave off such an unpleasant smell
and were so messy that an alternative had to be found. Beeswax
emitted a much more agreeable odor and was far less messy, so
it became a popular substitute for the tallow candles. More controversial were the candles made of whale spermaceti. This waxy
substance found in whale oil was popular because it burned slowly
and didn't melt in hot climates. As a result, many sperm whales
were killed for their spermaceti. Thankfully this trade has since
been banned.

A typical commercial candle contains 60 percent paraffin, 35
percent stearic acid, and 5 percent beeswax. Pure beeswax candles
only contain a small amount of paraffin and a stiffening agent—it is
this type of candle that we will now explore.

It's strange to think that the beeswax candles giving mood light
to your bathroom actually come from glands found on the abdomen

IT'S A FACT...

- It takes on average eleven hundred scales to create 0.04 ounces of wax.

- Candlemakers are traditionally known as chandlers.

- The origin of the expression "burning the candle at both ends" supposedly dates back to a time when candles were considered a luxury. Burning both ends therefore was seen as highly wasteful and extravagant.

- Ancient Egyptian philosophers and writers used early forms of candles to read and write by.

- Auctioneers used to use candles to time biddings. A pin would be inserted into the candle at a certain point so that when the flame reached that point, the pin would drop and the bidding would end.

- In 1874, Jean-Jacques Cambaraceres invented the first plaited wick that burned much more evenly than previous wicks.

- In order to produce wax, bees must consume large amounts of nectar (which they convert into honey as well as wax). Using long tubelike tongues, they suck the nectar from flowers and store it in separate honey-stomachs. It takes the nectar of up to 1,500 flowers to fill a bee's honey-stomach. To yield just one pound of beeswax bees must therefore fly about 150,000 miles.

- Candles stay alight through a series of self-sustaining events. The heat from the flame melts the top of the mass of solid fuel, the liquefied fuel then moves upward through the wick via capillary action, and the liquefied fuel is then vaporized to burn within the candle's flame.

of young worker bees. These glands secrete tiny transparent wax scales that are only a couple of millimeters across and 0.1 millimeter thick. The bees masticate the scales until they become opaque and waxy. They then use the wax to build honeycomb cells in which they house their young and store pollen. The pollen is what makes the wax turn that familiar yellow color. Bees start secreting wax when the temperature reaches higher than ninety degrees. Beekeepers then remove the wax from the honeycomb with a sharp uncapping knife. Any excess wax by-product, known as *slumgum*, is removed and discarded. The wax now needs to be rendered and purified so that it can be turned into candles.

Meanwhile, the wick is being made out of braided cotton or linen. The braiding helps create an even flame while the wick burns. The wick is then doused in fuel so that the candle flame stays alight for longer. Wicks are also treated with special chemicals that cause them to bend ninety degrees while burning. This keeps the wick firmly positioned in the flame's oxidizing zone.

The wax is placed into enormous kettles and heated until it

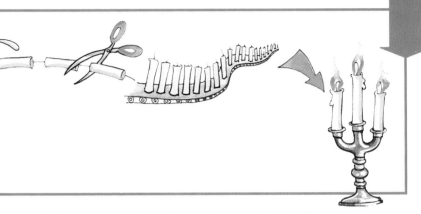

melts into a clear liquid. The molten wax is then filtered to remove any impurities. Dyes and perfumes are added where necessary. The wax is sent to molding machines, some of which are still operated by hand. However, these days most are automated and can churn out up to five hundred candles an hour. The wick is eased through the end of each mold, which is slightly tapered to help removal at the end of the process. The wax is cooled to just above melting point and then poured into heated molds that aid even distribution. Cold water is then poured into sleeves encasing the molds to help quicken the solidifying process. The hardened candle is removed from the mold leaving just enough wick for the next batch. In another method of candle-making called *extrusion*, paraffin wax is forced through a hot steel die at extreme pressure, producing a continuous snake of candle that is then cut to the desired lengths.

Rotating cutters taper the candle tips. They are now ready to be sent to an automated packing machine and then on to shops and churches across the world. From bee secretion to ambient lighting in just a few weeks . . . Let there be light!

This controversial confection receives a lot of bad press, as councils and governments across the world attempt to rid our streets of the sticky residue left by discarded gum. In Singapore, chewing gum has been banned and there are heavy fines—and even jail sentences—for those caught chewing. But human beings have always enjoyed the sensation of chewing something squishy. The Greeks chose mastic tree resin, while the Italians preferred the taste of frankincense. In Arabic countries people like to chew beeswax and in the West Indies, aromatic twigs. In America and Europe we prefer to chew sap from the spruce tree.

When you chew gum, you are in fact chewing a form of latex rubber. Although most manufacturers now use synthetic rubber, the sap from the tropical evergreen Manilkara chicle tree is still used in some high-end gum. Natural chewing gum is more expensive because the average chicle tree only produces about a quart of sap every four years. The most common synthetic latex used in gum these days is butadiene-styrene.

Although many manufacturers are keen to keep their recipes a closely guarded secret, the manufacturing process is pretty standard throughout the industry. So let's take a look at how natural gum is produced.

First, the latex from the chicle tree is harvested by workers who score the trees with a series of Xs. This allows the gooey chicle to flow down the grooves and into collecting vessels. The liquid latex is then strained to remove any tree residue and placed in large kettle drums, where it is boiled and reduced to two-thirds its original volume. The thickened latex mixture is sent to the chewing gum factory, where it is thoroughly mixed to make sure each batch is the same consistency. The gum is then placed in specially heated rooms and left to dry. Once hardened, the gum base is heated at

IT'S A FACT...

- A typical stick of gum contains 79 percent sugar or artificial sweeteners such as saccharine or aspartame.

- Fruit-flavored gum doesn't contain any trace of real fruit! For instance, apple flavor comes from ethyl acetate, and cherry flavor comes from benzaldehyde.

- Chewing gum is one of the only foodstuffs we don't actually swallow. So in effect, gum never actually gets consumed.

- The first sugar-based gum was patented in the United States in 1869 by a dentist! Sugarless gum only came into being in the mid 1970s.

- There are many types and flavors of gum. Wrigley's biggest sellers are Juicy Fruit, Double-mint, and Spearmint. Wrigley's also makes a chewing gum specially designed for people with dentures.

- The towering chicle tree can grow to over thirty yards tall!

a high temperature until it melts into a thick, sticky solution. The liquid is purified in high-speed centrifuges before being placed in casks where flavorings, corn syrup, and softening chemicals are added. Large metal blades stir the mixture until it is smooth and soft enough to be rolled out on a flat conveyor belt. Large kneading machines pummel the gum for several hours so that the finished product is extra-smooth and chewy.

Hunks of gum are then removed from the main source and rolled out until they reach the standard chewing gum thickness of 0.17 inches. A machine scores the sheet of gum into rectangular shapes. When the sheets harden to

IT'S A FACT...
The flavor from an average stick of gum lasts just five minutes.

the correct firmness, they are broken up
into sticks ready to be wrapped in foil or
grease-proof paper and shipped all over the
world (except Singapore, of course).

No one knows for sure which came first, the chicken or the egg, but one thing is certain, chicken remains the most popular and versatile meat in the world. And we have eggs to thank for that. Legs, thighs, breasts, innards, feet, claws, and even heads— there is very little of a chicken that isn't eaten somewhere in the world. In the United Kingdom and the United States, breast is best, closely followed by drumsticks and thighs. In Asia, chicken's feet are widely enjoyed, while in parts of Africa the head is considered a delicacy. Controversy about animal welfare still surrounds mass-market chicken production, but as long as the meat remains popular, large-scale battery farming (a method which confines hens to cages and first appeared back in the 1920s) is sure to continue.

So how does a muddy egg end up as a plump, juicy chicken on your dinner table? Regrettably, life for the average hen is not a happy one. It begins with severe overcrowding and ends with a ritualistic beheading.

Broiler chickens begin life in a hatchery. The fertilized eggs are collected from chicken coops where breeder hens have been hard at work laying the raw material (once they've laid, the breeders are sent to the slaughterhouse, where they end up in processed soups and pet food—there's gratitude for you!).

Hatchery workers meanwhile transfer the eggs onto special trolleys and wheel them directly into a giant temperature- and humidity-controlled incubator. The yolk, egg white, and shell nourish the embryo as it grows inside the incubator. Once every hour, the trays containing the eggs automatically shift forty-five degrees to the left and then back again, mimicking the way hens turn their eggs before hatching. Exactly eighteen-and-a-half days later, the eggs are removed from the incubator and placed on a conveyor belt, where an infrared detector checks for any unfertilized eggs that may have slipped through by mistake. A special suction machine automatically removes the unfertilized eggs, which are sent off to become animal feed. The fertilized eggs continue along the conveyor belt to the next stage of the process. Automated needles pierce the eggs and inject the amniotic fluid surrounding the chick with a vaccine to protect the growing fetus against Marek's Disease, a common illness among chickens.

Another suction machine transfers the vaccinated eggs to hatching trays that hold exactly 168 eggs per tray. Only about 150 of these eggs will go on to hatch; the rest are either prematurely dead or severely deformed. On day nineteen, the chicks begin to hatch by using their beaks to peck through the shell. It usually takes about six hours for the exhausted chick to finally emerge into the world (little does the poor creature know the fate that awaits it). As soon as they are born, chicks are able to see and walk. They

are covered in a layer of soft downy feathers. Hundreds of chicks are then taken in trolleys to a *separator*, a moving device that separates the chicks from the open shells. Because the chicks are smaller than the shells, they tumble through gaps in the machine and onto another moving conveyor belt below. The discarded shells are sent to a rendering plant. The chicks meanwhile continue along the conveyor belt toward several workers who are waiting to separate them out according to gender. The only way the workers can tell the birds apart is by checking the feathers. Females have two rows of feathers at different heights whereas males have feathers all the same size. The workers sift through the piles of chicks, sending the females down one chute and the males down another. It looks cruel and probably is. Both chutes feed a different conveyor belt where an optical counter keeps track of numbers. The separated chicks fall into either a male or female transportation box that holds exactly 102 birds. The chicks are then sprayed with an

CHICKEN DINNER

anti-bronchitis vaccine before being sent to
the grow-out farm, a gigantic hangar that can
hold more than twenty thousand birds at any one time. Some farmers choose to de-beak their hens at this stage to prevent them from
injuring each other, but most now agree the practice is cruel and
unnecessary—hens, after all, tend to be quite passive birds.

Because of severe overcrowding, each chick has less than a
square foot of space in which to live and feed. Their diet consists
of corn and soy with added vitamins and minerals to help fatten
them up. The female chicks will reach slaughtering age after about
thirty-eight days, whereas the males can take between forty and
sixty-five days. Due to the intense feeding methods, the chickens
very quickly balloon in size. Many become so fat that they can
hardly stand. But things are about to get a whole lot worse . . . our
plump, fully grown chickens are now ready for the slaughterhouse.
This is where it gets gruesome. The birds are collected at night

(when they are at their most docile). Some farmers quite literally suck the chickens out of the hanger with a large vacuum-cleaner-like device. Others simply round up the chickens by hand and place them in boxes ready to be transported to the processing plant.

Let's follow the progress of a single chicken—we'll call her Hilda. When Hilda arrives at the plant she is immediately hung upside down from a moving conveyor belt. From here she passes through a *stun cabinet* full of electrified salt water, where she will remain for about seven seconds. (Those of a nervous disposition should look away now!) From here our paralyzed bird is moved to an automatic neck-cutting machine, where rotating blades sever the carotid artery in the neck. The headless carcass is left to hang until all the blood has drained away. (Still looking forward to that Sunday roast?) The bloodless corpse is then immersed in boiling water, which scalds the skin and softens the feathers, making them easier to remove. Automatic feather-pickers scrape away all the loose feathers. The head, feet, and internal organs are removed and the insides thoroughly cleaned of any last traces of yuck. (Okay, you can start reading again now.) The washed carcass is sent down a chute into a vat of chilled chlorinated water. When the carcass reaches forty degrees or below, Hilda's remains are taken in a large container stuffed with hundreds of other carcasses to the cutting area. A trained assembly line of cutters and deboners places each chicken, bottom first, onto a cone-shaped stand. This frees up their hands for the gruesome job ahead. Each worker is given an exceptionally sharp knife. The wings are removed first using a quick downward motion along the inside of each wing where it joins the body. The workers then peel the skin off the carcass and remove both breasts in one clean movement. The breasts are separated and checked for bones.

The wings are transferred to a small revolving wheel called a wing-cutter. Sharp knives cut each wing into three sections—the meaty drumettes, the not-so-meaty winglet, and the virtually meatless wing tip. The winglets and tips are piled inside a large revolving drum that coats them in seasoning. They are then placed in an oven and cooked for approximately ten minutes at 482 degrees Fahrenheit. The cooked wings are bagged and sold as "buffalo wings." The breasts and drumsticks are either deep fried, frozen, or sold raw so that the consumer can cook 'em just the way he or she likes 'em. Of course, many chickens are left whole for broiling.

If you care about animal well-being, always buy free-range chickens—even though they do still end up having their heads chopped off.

Humans have some peculiar habits, but burning dried leaves and then inhaling the smoke they create has to be one of the strangest.

When Christopher Columbus arrived in the New World, he found the locals enjoyed rolling up tobacco leaves and smoking them. He was so taken by the idea that he brought a shipment of the exotic new plant back to Europe—and so the idea of the cigar as we know it was born. Although cigar smoking initially became popular among sailors, the rest of the world didn't really catch on until the end of the eighteenth century, when cigar factories started appearing across Spain, Germany, and France. During the Napoleonic Wars, English officers brought cigars back home and the habit soon became popular among the upper classes, although it remained strictly a male pursuit.

Cigar smoking went out of favor after World War II, but it became fashionable again in the 1990s, especially among rich businessmen and Hollywood actors.

Although Cuba still makes the finest cigars, other countries such as the Philippines, Java, Russia, and Sri Lanka also have a thriving cigar industry. The United States has factories in Pennsylvania, Connecticut, New York, and Florida.

So how do you turn a bunch of withered old leaves into one of the world's most potent status symbols? Well, the main ingredient in cigars is, of course, the tobacco leaf. There are three types of tobacco leaves used in the manufacturing of cigars: the large, finely textured outer leaf, or *wrapper*; the inner leaves, known as *binders* hold everything in place; and the shredded leaves, which are used as *fillers*. The wrapper leaves come from the widest part of the plant and give the cigar its look, character, and pungent aroma. A combination of different strengths of filler give the desired flavor or *blend*. Depending on the quality of the cigar, the fillers are made

IT'S A FACT...

- The most expensive cigars in the world cost $429 each or $18,846 for a box of forty. They are called *Behike*, an ancient Colombian word meaning sorcerer, doctor, or priest. Why would anyone want to burn something so valuable?

- The world record for the longest hand-rolled cigar is held by master cigar maker Wally Reyes, who in 2006 rolled a cigar 101 feet long and one inch in diameter. The raw materials cost $3,500. Reyes was assisted by his wife and fourteen specially trained volunteers.

- Well-known cigar smokers include Winston Churchill, Groucho Marx, and Al Capone. Churchill reputedly went through ten cigars a day.

- Cigars used to be given as prizes in fairground shooting games, hence the expression "close but no cigar" when someone missed the target.

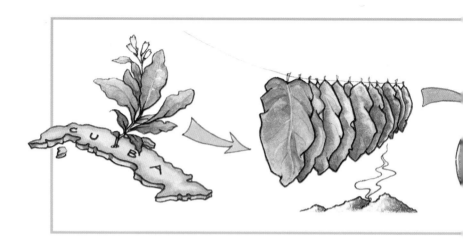

either from shredded whole leaves or a combination of leaves and stems. The finest and most expensive cigars only use leaves from high-quality plants, whereas less expensive varieties may use high-quality outer leaves and cheaper binders and fillers.

The tobacco plants are initially grown in large indoor warehouses, but after about ten weeks they are transferred to fields. Regular pruning ensures the plants grow to a healthy size. During growth the valuable outer leaves need to be shielded from the sun with a protective covering. After about six months, the bright green leaves begin to turn

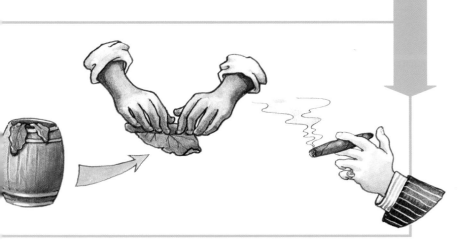

brown (a result of the chlorophyll breaking down), meaning they are mature enough to be harvested. The leaves are removed, often by hand, and then taken to curing barns, where they are attached to wooden strips called *laths* and suspended from the ceiling. The leaves are either left to dry naturally in well-ventilated barns or *flu-cured* in smaller heated barns where the temperature can reach over ninety degrees Fahrenheit. To add flavor and to help the leaves dry, sawdust is sometimes left on the floor of the curing barns.

Once the leaves have been cured, they are sorted by size and color and then made into bundles known as *hands*. Each hand contains between ten and fifteen leaves. The hands are then placed in casks known as *hogsheads* and left to ferment for up to five years. The higher the quality of tobacco, the longer the hands are left to ferment and the richer the eventual taste and aroma will be. After fermentation, skilled workers sort through the leaves by hand.

The leaves are now ready to be assembled. First, all stems must be removed from the filler leaves so that the cigar will burn evenly. To do this, a worker attaches a thimble knife to his or her finger and strips away the main stem, which runs down the center of the leaf. The stemless leaves are then stacked in piles known in the trade as *books*.

Mass-produced cigars are rolled in factories, but the fine cigars are still rolled by hand. Hand rolling is a highly skilled job that can take more than a year to master. The roller must evenly distribute the filler throughout the cigar, while making sure the outer leaves spiral evenly around the filler—this will ensure that the cigar burns at the correct speed. Professional rollers must first select between two and six filler leaves (depending on the size of the cigar) and roll them into a tight bundle. The bundle of filler leaves is placed on the binder leaf and rolled into a cylindrical shape. The cigars are then held in wooden molds ready to be wrapped. This is where the roller's skill really comes into play, ensuring the cigar is wrapped to the right tightness. The roller places the cigar filling onto the wrapper leaf and, with a sharp knife called a *chaveta*, trims away any loose, unsightly bits of leaf. Traditionally the outer leaf is rolled exactly three-and-a-half times around the filling. The roller then seals the end with a dab of vegetable paste. A small circle of leaf about the size of a coin is cut and then pasted to the open end.

The finished cigar is now ready for quality inspection. Strict examiners check for consistency, appearance, and quality of roll. As with all high-quality products, the mastery is in the detail. For example, the veins of the wrapping must all point in exactly the same direction in order to form a uniform spiral. It's also important that the outer leaves remain smooth and taut.

Once the cigars have passed quality control, specialists sort them into their various shades—each box must contain exactly the same shade of cigar. Finally, a banding machine places a paper band with the manufacturer's logo around the top of each cigar. The finished masterpieces are then packed into metal tubes or wooden boxes, ready to be enjoyed at home, in cigar bars, or any celebratory setting.

Next time you grapple with a condom, try not to think about the remarkable journey it has made to get from wood to *wood.*

Condoms are made from natural rubbers. Ironically, every condom begins its life as gooey, spermlike sap inside the bark of a hard, erect tree.

Latex is a mixture of organic compounds produced in special cells called *laticifers.* The molecules of the rubber within these tiny tubes consist of five carbon and eight hydrogen atoms. These molecules are linked together to form long, chainlike molecules called *polymers.* It is this linking formation that gives rubber its elasticity (which is incredibly useful when attempting to pull a condom on in the dark and your mind is on other things).

Most natural rubber comes from a single species of tree, Hevea Brasiliensis. Though native to South America, these trees can also be found on large plantations in Southeast Asia and take about three years to mature. Spiraling grooves are cut around each tree trunk, allowing the liquid latex to run down into special collection cups. Thousands of workers, known as *rubber tappers*, collect the liquid latex and flatten it into sheets, using their bare feet. The sheets are then hung out to dry.

Once the latex has passed through quality control, it needs to be processed into a useable form. Latex is a naturally occurring substance similar to milk in many of its physical properties—it can curdle or spoil if not treated. In a process known as *compounding,* stabilizers, preservatives, and vulcanizing agents are added, and the latex is inspected for quality and consistency.

The next stage, known as *dipping,* involves feeding the compound latex into temperature-controlled tanks. Glass *formers* (erect penis–shaped molds) dip into the tanks, where they receive an extremely thin film of latex. This coating is dried using filtered air

IT'S A FACT...

▶ Breakage rates for condoms used in the United States are less than 2 percent while in the UK it's closer to 4 percent.

▶ The first published use of the word "condum" was in a poem written in 1706. It has also been suggested that Condom was the name of a doctor working for Charles II. He apparently invented the device to prevent the king from having any more illegitimate children.

▶ Condoms are also known as rubbers, French letters, raincoats, love gloves, jimmy hats, and wrappers.

▶ The rubber tappers of the South American rain forest, known as seringueiros, get paid 60 cents a day.

▶ Interesting fact about rubber: Every year, car tires shed more than eighty thousand tons of rubber on U.S. roads. Surprisingly, very little trace of this rubber fallout is ever found. This is because microorganisms living by the roadside find the taste of rubber irresistible and consume it in vast amounts.

▶ Durex is the bestselling condom in the world. The name Durex derives from the words: "durability," "reliability," and "excellence." In 1982 the company decided to drop the size small condoms because no one was buying them.

to prevent atmospheric contamination. Once dry, the formers are dipped again and then dried again.

When the dipping process is complete, the open ends are rolled over to form a rim. While still on the formers, the condoms pass through an oven to vulcanize the latex before being removed by high-pressure jets of water.

The finished condoms undergo stringent safety tests to ensure perfection and reliability. Each condom is stretched over a metal former and subjected to a high-voltage electric shock (ouch!). The latex is then examined for flaws. Even the most microscopic damage will mean the

IT'S A FACT...

Every time you put on a condom, you are in fact rolling tree sap down your penis!

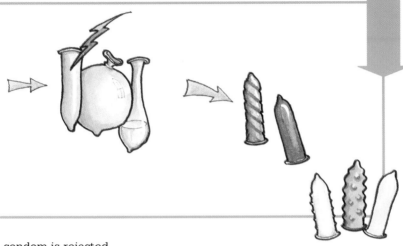

condom is rejected.

Random batches of condoms are also filled with air to check for holes. Typically, a condom can hold 1.4 cubic feet of air before bursting. These same batches are then filled with water (about 1.25 cups) and suspended for three minutes before being rolled across sheets of blotting paper to check for leakage. If any condom shows signs of water loss, the entire batch will be rejected.

More samples are checked for size, thickness, and physical strength, while others will be artificially aged to see how they fare at the end of the standard five-year guarantee.

Before being shipped to pharmacies and specialty shops across the world, the condoms are doused in Nonoxynol-9 spermicide and hermetically sealed inside a rectangular aluminium-foil pouch. Whether you like flavored, studded, glow-in-the-dark, or extra large, there's a condom for every desire.

The humble crayon is loved by children everywhere. But there was a time when children wouldn't have been allowed anywhere near crayons because of their high toxicity levels. The first crayons, as used in early cave paintings, were made of carbon sticks left over from fires. In the nineteenth century, black crayons were used in factories as waterproof markers for barrels and crates. Colored crayons were invented soon after, but were unsuitable for children because they contained toxic materials such as charcoal.

Modern crayons are made of paraffin wax, a by-product of petroleum that is both inexpensive and easy to melt. Paraffin wax also has what's known as a good *rub-off*, meaning it leaves just the right amount of wax on paper after it is pressed down. While the paraffin wax is transported to the crayon factory, it must be kept in liquid form in specially heated trucks. Meanwhile, over at the crayon factory, pigments are crushed into powder form, ready to be mixed with the hot wax. Pigments used to come from natural substances such as dead beetles, plants, animal waste, and mollusks, but most are made from synthetic materials.

The powdery pigments are mixed in large wooden tanks and forced through filters to remove any excess water. They are then placed in kilns and dried for several days. The dry lumps of pigment are divided up into their different colors, crushed to a powder again, and then blended to make sure the colors are consistent. Meanwhile, the paraffin is pumped into huge supply tanks that can hold up to seventeen thousand gallons of liquid. The wax is blended with the pigments and some powdered filler in smaller heated vessels for about forty-five minutes. Fatty acids are also added to improve the rub-off. The wax is then pumped into a giant rotary machine that forces the wax into crayon-shaped molds. The

IT'S A FACT...

- During the 1990s, a range of scented crayons became available. Kids loved the aroma of apple and strawberry so much that they started eating the crayons. As a result, the crayon company changed the names of the scents to non-food aromas, although, because crayons are non-toxic, parents didn't have to worry.

- There are more than one hundred different colors of crayon available.

- The first non-toxic colored crayons were produced in 1903.

- Crayola, the world's biggest manufacturer of crayons, produces almost three billion crayons each year. Invented by cousins Edwin Binney and C. Harold Smith, the brand's first box of eight crayons retailed for a nickel. Alice Stead Binney, wife of Edwin Binney, came up with the name Crayola by combining the French words "craie," meaning chalk, and "oleaginous," meaning oily. Today, Crayola produces a whole range of crayons, including ones that sparkle, glow in the dark, smell of flowers, and change color.

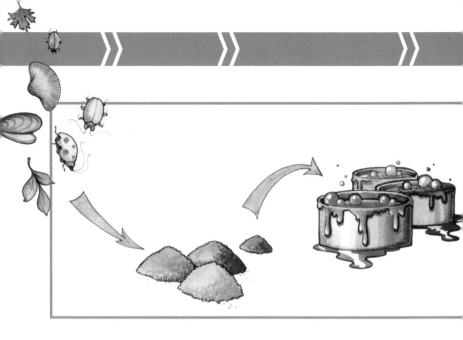

molds are doused with cold water to harden the wax in less than a minute. As the molds continue along a conveyor belt, the excess wax is scraped off and recycled. Each rotary machine can produce more than 2,700 crayons per cycle. Some colors take longer to cool than others, but each hardened crayon is inspected for breakage and bubbling.

The finished crayons are placed into racks, ready to be labeled. As well as showing the manufacturer's logo, the paper labels also protect the delicate crayons while they're in transit. Automated machines drop the finished

IT'S A FACT...
One color, Indian yellow, used to be produced by collecting the urine of cows fed exclusively on mango leaves!

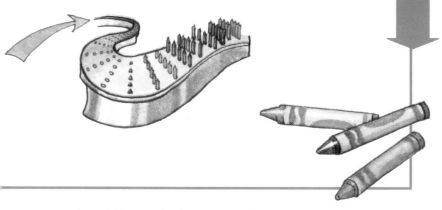

crayons into different-size boxes ready for shipping. Because of the high demand and the many different colors produced (more than a hundred in some factories), crayon machines keep running day and night to produce an average of thirty thousand crayons an hour.

Where would Homer Simpson be without his daily diet of delicious donuts (with extra sprinkles, of course)? As our donut-(or should that be *d'oh!*-nut) loving hero famously once said, "Is there anything they can't do?" Well, in truth the only thing donuts are really any good at is being eaten, but the journey from dough to donut is certainly a fascinating one.

Opinion is divided on the origin of donuts. Evidence suggests that Dutch settlers introduced them to the United States in the mid-nineteenth century. Back then, donuts were called *olykoeks*— a Dutch word meaning oily cake. There is also evidence that donut-shaped pastries were eaten by prehistoric Native Americans in the Southwest. But it was an American by the name of Hansen Gregory who claimed to have come up with the idea of the ring donut back in 1847. Our hero was only sixteen at the time, and on board a lime-trading ship bound for home. Bored with the heftiness of olykoeks, he began punching out the greasy centers, leaving just the light outer ring of dough. Back on dry land, his mother was so impressed she set to work making a batch for her friends. Word quickly spread.

So how are modern donuts actually made? Our journey begins inside an actual donut store. Thankfully, these tasty treats are often made on-site rather than in a factory. Every day, the donut store receives a shipment of special recipe yeast from the manufacturer. Workers mix the yeast with water to form a brew, which is left to circulate in a large metal container for two hours. The light, fluffy mixture is then poured into a mixing drum and churned for exactly twelve minutes.

The thick, gooey dough is transferred to a trough where it is left to breathe for ten minutes—this is called *floor time* in the trade. The dough is now ready to be dropped into an *extruder*. This

IT'S A FACT...

▶ The world record for donut eating is held not by Homer Simpson but by John Haight, who in 1981 consumed twenty-nine donuts in just over six minutes.

▶ The first printed use of the word "donut" was seen in an article in the *Los Angeles Times* on August 10, 1929.

▶ The largest jelly donut ever made weighed a whopping 1.9 tons. Created in Utica, New York, on January 21, 1993, it measured sixteen feet in diameter and was sixteen inches thick in the center.

machine exerts a downward pressure on the dough, causing it to ooze out of eight circular holes situated in the base of the extruder. The size and shape of each donut depends on how much pressure is exerted.

The raw dough shells are now placed on moving shelves inside a large oven called a *proof box*, which is heated to 124 degrees Fahrenheit. As the dough shells move around the hot oven, the

yeast causes them to rise gradually. After about forty minutes, the now puffy donuts are automatically dropped into a moving channel of vegetable oil heated to 360 degrees. As they float along, the hot oil cooks the underside. Halfway along the channel, an automatic flipping machine turns each donut over so that both sides are cooked equally.

The whole frying process only takes about two minutes, or one minute per side. The cooked donuts move out of the hot oil and onto another conveyor belt for drying. They pass under a luxurious waterfall of sweet liquid glaze made of sugar, water, and a stabilizer. Another conveyor belt transports the glazed donuts directly into the

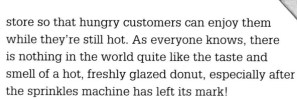

store so that hungry customers can enjoy them
while they're still hot. As everyone knows, there
is nothing in the world quite like the taste and
smell of a hot, freshly glazed donut, especially after
the sprinkles machine has left its mark!

For filled donuts, the workers remove the empty shells from the
conveyor belt before they reach the shop floor. Each donut is individually pushed onto a nozzle attached to a plastic container full
of jelly or cream filling. As the nozzle enters the donut, two gears
inside the bottle measure out an exact dollop so that each donut
receives the same amount of gooey gorgeousness. The freshly
filled donuts then pass along another conveyor belt either directly
into the store or into the packing area, where workers fill dozens of
boxes ready to be shipped. Some on-site donut stores can produce
up to sixty thousand donuts a day—just don't tell Homer Simpson.

Glass—the perfect combination of sand, gypsum, soda ash,
limestone, and dolomite—is a remarkable substance that can be
molded into almost any shape. But how do you turn dense, non-
transparent geological material into fragile, see-through glass?

Before we visit the bottle factory, let's have a look at how glass
is made. Glass begins its life in the mineral mines of America,
where the raw ingredients are found. Once sand and other ingredients have been quarried, they are sent directly to the glass factory
by rail or truck. Conveyor belts transport each material to giant
silos. The minerals are then weighed and sent to the melting furnace. Sand (or *silica*, as it is officially known) makes up more than
50 percent of the finished glass and usually only melts at a scorching three thousand degrees Fahrenheit. But when mixed with other
minerals, silica liquefies at a slightly less scorching two thousand
degrees. Broken recycled glass, known as *cullet,* is then added to
the mixture—this lowers the batch's melting point to a more stable
1,600 degrees. Giant fans force hot air into the furnace. The hot
air combines with jets of natural gas to produce great flames that
fan out over the batch, causing it to melt in just a few minutes.
The amazing thing about silica is that when it becomes liquid, the
molecules separate and allow light to pass through, which is what
gives glass its transparent quality.

The molten glass, now the consistency of honey, is then allowed
to breathe. Trapped air bubbles rise to the surface and are released
into the furnace's atmosphere. The liquid glass passes through a
canal into the forming chamber. This is where the deep river of
molten glass is transformed into clear flat panes. During what's
known as the *bath process,* the hardened glass is broken down
into chunks and moved into another furnace containing molten tin.
Because liquid glass is less dense than tin, it spreads out across

the surface to form a perfectly flat sheet of glass. The panes are slowly cooled in cooling ovens until they reach room temperature. If the glass cools too quickly, it becomes brittle and shatters. The finished panes are now ready to be scored and cut into useable sizes. Because so many sheets of glass are produced each day (more than thirty miles in some factories), the whole manufacturing process happens very fast. So it's vital that the cut glass is removed quickly from the cutting area, as more sheets are arriving all the time. One mistimed pane could literally shatter a whole day's work!

Meanwhile, over at the bottle factory, tubes of molten glass flow from a furnace down long chutes. Strategically placed shears cut the lengths at precise intervals, producing smaller, bottle-sized gobs that drop down into a device called a *scoop*. The scoop moves the gobs to a large trough and on to the bottle-forming machines. Here each gob is forced into a preliminary mold. A few seconds later, they emerge as miniature bottle shapes. From here the solid

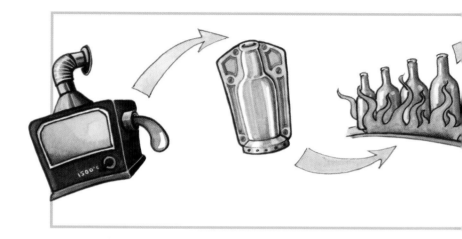

shapes are placed in blow molds that are the size and shape of the finished bottle. Compressed air is blown into the mold, hollowing out the glass center to form the finished bottle shape. The bottles then leave the forming machine and travel along a conveyor belt full of flames. The heat from the flames ensures the glass doesn't cool down too quickly and break from thermal shock. A loading machine pushes the bottles into a large, temperature-controlled cooling area. As they move slowly through the area, the bottles are sprayed with lubricant to aid the inspection process. The bottles are then channeled into single file where an automated inspection machine spins each bottle to check for imperfections. Cameras search for cracks and bubbles. Each bottle receives a final visual inspection from a factory worker before being packaged and sent out to beer, wine, liquor, and soft drink manufacturers.

But there is still one mystery—how does glass remain transparent even when cooled? Well, glass has a unique, almost magical

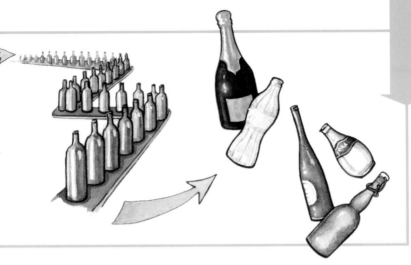

quality—it never crystallizes, which means it never actually becomes solid! That's why when you look at old windows, the panes of glass appear thicker at the bottom than at the top—the liquid panes are slowly moving with the pull of gravity! When ordinary liquid is cooled to below its melting point, it usually solidifies. But glass remains a liquid even if it falls below its melting point.

Without glue, so many objects we now take for granted would simply fall apart. Furniture, shoes, buildings, and cars all rely on adhesives to hold them together. This book would be a pile of loose pages without the help of the sticky stuff. Strange to think that such a vital component of modern life actually comes from dead animals!

Early hunter-gatherers discovered that various animal remains—such as bones, skin, blood, muscle sinew, fish bones, scales, skin, and the lining of a fish's air bladder—all contained a gloopy substance called *collagen* that can be used to stick stuff together. Collagen is still used in the manufacturing of glue, but how is all that yucky bone and sinew turned into clear, strong adhesive?

Our journey begins in the slaughterhouse. The world's largest glue factory is in fact part of a huge dairy farm called Borden Company. Animal remains such as ears, tails, tendons, bones, and feet are transported from the farm's slaughterhouse to the glue factory, where they are first cleaned and then soaked in order to make the parts good and soft. The resulting *stock*, as it is known, then passes through a series of water baths. Lime is added to the water to make the various animal by-products swell and break down. The parts are then transferred to large revolving washing machines.

Hydrochloric acid is added to dissolve any last traces of lime before the animal parts are transferred to open tanks full of boiling water, which breaks down the collagen and converts it to a sticky solution. Massive steam coils in the tanks heat the water to exactly 160 degrees Fahrenheit—if the temperature or timing is wrong, the glue will be spoiled. The thick, opaque collagen is then passed through three more tanks of increasingly hot water. The resulting

IT'S A FACT...

- Glue is officially a dairy by-product.

- The average U.S. citizen uses around fifty pounds of glue a year.

- Surgeons believe that in the future many open wounds will be held together with glue rather than stitches.

- Curdled milk and cow's blood were used by primitive man as early forms of adhesive.

- Traces of glue have been found in ancient cave paintings in Lascaux, France.

- Mussels have a natural adhesive on their "feet" that is even stronger than super-glue.

- 50,000 years ago Neanderthal man made glue out of birch bark.

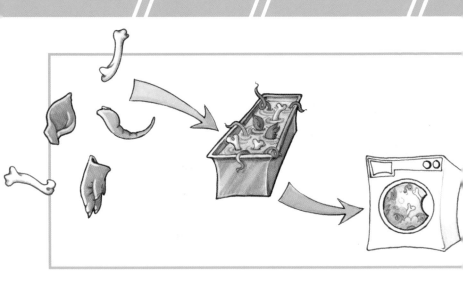

liquid, known as *glue liquor*, is removed and heated again until it thickens.

When left to cool, the substance becomes solid and jellylike. Acids and egg albumin are added to thin the glue and remove any impurities. The runny glue is cleaned by passing it through a filter of ground-up bone known as *bone char*. To give the glue just the right consistency, the liquid is concentrated in vacuum evaporators before being chilled into sheets or blocks and suspended in nets to dry. The blocks are now ready to be softened and pumped into tubes and jars.

Just think, without all those yucky animal remains,

there would be no couches to sit on, no TVs to watch, no computer screens to work at, and no *Hew, Screw, and Glue* to read! Take a look around you—it's amazing how many things rely on glue for their survival.

Arguments still rage about the origin of the hot dog. The city of Frankfurt, Germany, claims to have invented the frankfurter back in 1852, but some argue that it was Johann Georghehner, a butcher from Coburg, Germany, who came up with the idea of the "dachshund" sausage (similar in look and texture to a frankfurter) in the 1600s.

Rumor has it that frankfurters became known as "dogs" because they were originally made out of dog meat! Well, that's certainly not true these days . . .

Sausages, in one form or another, have remained a popular staple food for many thousands of years. There is evidence that they were eaten in Babylon as far back as 1500 BCE. The great thinker and poet Homer even mentions sausages in his masterwork *The Odyssey*.

The very first sausages were made of animal intestine stuffed with offal—it doesn't sound so great, but apparently once they'd been cooked over an open fire they weren't too bad.

In 1871, Charles Feltman and Antoine Feuchtwanger introduced "wiener" sausages to America. Feltman famously wrapped his sausages in milk rolls, smothered them in mustard and sauerkraut, and began selling them from a stand situated on Coney Island. It was here that the legendary "hot dog" was born.

Pork is traditionally the main ingredient in hot dogs, although chicken, beef, and turkey have become popular in recent years. Let's follow the journey of a typical pork dog. As with any pork product, the journey begins with the humble pig. Once a pig reaches maturity, it is slaughtered and then divided up into various cuts, such as bacon, pork chops, and ham. Contrary to popular belief, hot dogs are not made from unwanted leftover meat such as snout, testicles, and ears. In fact, the U.S. Department of Agriculture specifies that only trimmings from high-grade cuts can be used

IT'S A FACT...

▸ A typical peeling machine peels 700 hot dogs a minute!

▸ Hot dogs are also known as wieners, frankfurters, red-hots, rippers, franks, mini-sausages, ballparks, and dachshunds.

▸ More than sixteen billion hot dogs are consumed in the United States each year.

▸ Pinks, established in Los Angeles in 1939, is one of the oldest family-run hot dog stands in the United States.

▸ July is National Hot Dog Month.

▸ Hot dogs became the standard cuisine for baseball games back in 1893.

in sausage products. Sometimes offal such as liver may be added, but this has to be clearly labeled as "variety meats." All meat is made up of various chemicals that give it distinctive qualities. For example, myoglobin and hemoglobin proteins give meat color, myofibrillar adds texture, and fat gives distinctive flavors.

So now the pork cuts are ready to be sent to the hot dog factory for processing. After the meat has been inspected for quality, it is sent through a metal meat grinder full of graded holes. The ground meat is mixed in a vat along with curing ingredients (to increase shelf life), food starch (that thickens the mix), salt, and binders and fillers (such as breadcrumbs, cereal, and oatmeal). The mixture is then sprayed with water and poured into a large rectangular vat where revolving blades grind the meat until it becomes a smooth, homogenous batter. A dash of corn syrup gives it some sweetness, and more water is added to make the finished wieners

extra juicy. The gooey mixture is then forced through tubes into a stuffing machine that pumps the meat into a long collagen casing (some manufacturers prefer natural casings made from sheep intestines that give the familiar *snap* when bitten into). The casing is twisted every five-and-a-quarter inches (the length of a hot dog) to form a continual snake of linked sausages. It takes just thirty-five seconds to make a chain of sausages twice the length of a soccer field. Three of these long chains are linked together to form a much longer chain that is then fed through a machine that drapes them over moving racks. The racks pass the links through a liquid smoke shower and on to an oven with several different cooking zones. During the baking process, the smoky liquid seeps through the casing, adding flavor to the wieners.

The cooked franks are then sprayed with very cold, salty water, which chills them so that they are ready for packaging. The dogs file down into an unloading zone. A machine removes them from

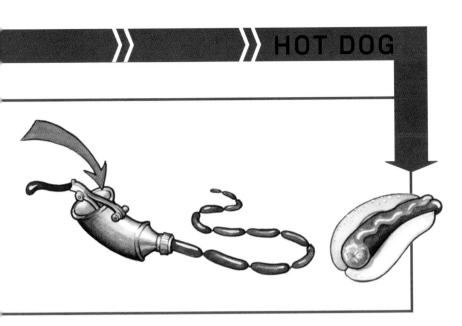

the racks and onto a conveyor that looks a bit like a hot dog high-way, where a peeling machine cuts along each casing. The casings are then blown off with a hot jet of steam.

Inspectors check that all the casings have been removed. A machine that looks like a plastic bicycle chain with sprockets positions the wieners for packaging. Three hundred thousand wieners are produced an hour, which is about two-and-a-half million per shift! The finished wieners are laid out on sheets of plastic in groups of six or eight, ready to be packaged. The sheets are then folded around the dogs and vacuum-sealed for freshness. Small amounts of saline may be added to help preserve the meat. The succulent wieners are now ready to be burned to a cinder at summer barbecues across the land.

Next time you sink your teeth into a juicy frank, remember: It's not easy being a sausage . . .

Happy eating, dachshund-lovers!

Up until the beginning of the nineteenth century, mankind had only two sources of light—fire and the sun. So imagine how miraculous it must have been when Sir Humphrey Davy came up with his remarkable man-made light source known as the "incandescent electric light." The world could now enjoy instant light at the flick of a switch.

Lightbulbs were first mass-produced back in the 1920s. They now come in all sorts of shapes and sizes, from tiny flashlight bulbs to fluorescent tubes to enormous lighthouse bulbs. So how do bits of glass and wire end up illuminating whole cities?

The most important part of a lightbulb is a thin piece of wire known as a filament. Filaments are made from *tungsten*, an incredibly durable metal that has the highest melting point (6,192 degrees Fahrenheit) and the highest tensile strength of all the elements. This super-strong metal is therefore ideal for creating white heat, the basis of all man-made heat. Making tungsten wire involves a process called *drawing* in which the metal is mixed with a binder and pulled through a narrow die to form an exceptionally thin wire. The wire is then wound around a metal bar known as a *mandrel* to form a coil. The coil is heated until it becomes soft—this process is called *annealing*. The redundant mandrel is then dissolved in acid. Tiny hooks attach the lead-in wires (that will eventually connect the bulb to the electrical source) to the filament. The lead-in wires hold the precious tungsten wire securely in place right at the heart of the glass casing.

Meanwhile over at the bulb factory two production lines are running concurrently—one produces the glass casings and the other the metal bases.

Once the melted glass has been removed from the furnace it is sent through a ribbon machine that produces a continuous strip of

IT'S A FACT...

- Most tungsten deposits are found in China.

- Ribbon machines can produce over fifty thousand bulbs an hour.

- Depending on wattage, the average lifespan of a lightbulb is between 750 and 1,000 hours. When the tungsten eventually burns itself out, it leaves a dark deposit on the glass known as "bulb-wall blackening."

- World tungsten reserves have been estimated at seven million tons, which means at current rates of consumption, these reserves will only last for about another 140 years.

- The word tungsten comes from the Swedish words *tung* and *sten* meaning heavy stone.

- Less than three percent of the input energy of a lightbulb is converted into usable light. The rest ends up as heat. Incandescent light bulbs are therefore gradually being phased out because of their inefficiency.

- About 45,00 tons of tungsten is mined each year.

red-hot glass. As the strip moves along a conveyor belt, strategically placed air nozzles positioned below blow the gobs of glass through holes in the conveyor belt directly into bulb-shaped molds above. The newly formed glass casings are removed from the mold, left to cool, and then cut into individual units. The casings either remain as clear glass or are sprayed with an interior coating of silica that reduces glare.

The aluminum bases meanwhile are being formed inside screw-shaped molds. The leader wires and tungsten filament are fitted to the base along with a glass exhaust tube that removes the air from the casing. Pressurized argon gas is then pumped into the casing through the glass pipe. Argon is an inert gas that resists heat build-up, ensuring the filament doesn't burn out too quickly. Torches then melt and seal off the exhaust tube, locking in the argon gas. The casing is now ready to be fitted to the aluminum base. The lead wires that will carry the electrical current from the light socket are soldered into place, one on the side, the other on the base. On the way to the packaging area the bulbs undergo what's known as *flash testing* where they are subjected to repeated light-ups using a higher voltage each time. This strengthens the filament. The extreme temperatures give an idea of how long the bulb will last under normal circumstances. The bulbs are now placed on a large revolving wheel that tests them one last

time to make sure they haven't broken on the way to the packing area. An automated packing machine gently separates the bulbs into pairs ready to be boxed.

Hope that sheds some light on how light is shed!

"God hath given you one face and you make yourself another"—
so said Hamlet to Ophelia in one of his darker moments. But
makeup, and especially lip color, has been a popular female
adornment for thousands of years. It was first used in Mesopotamia more than five thousand years ago, when women would
grind down brightly colored semi-precious stones and apply the
powder to their lips and eyelids. Over in Egypt, Cleopatra made
lipstick out of crushed ants and the luscious red pigment found
in carmine beetles. In the sixteenth century, Queen Elizabeth I
made lip color fashionable with her striking black lipstick comprised of beeswax and plant extracts. By the eighteenth century,
however, lipstick had lost its gloss. Many considered it to be
the devil's work, an evil scourge designed to excite and ensnare
men. In 1770, British Parliament even passed a law stating that
"women found guilty of seducing men into matrimony by cosmetic means could be tried for witchcraft." After Queen Victoria
condemned lipstick as "impolite," people began to associate
this once fashionable adornment with prostitutes and "loose"
women. Lipstick only became popular again during World War
II, when glamorous actresses were seen wearing it in movies.
These days, lipstick is as popular as ever. The style and range of
colors is vast.

So, how do you turn the raw ingredients of wax, pigments, oils,
and alcohol into the world's favorite facial adornment? First, all
the raw materials need to be melted, mixed, and then heated in
separate steel containers. The oils are mixed with the color pigments and passed through a roller mill, where the pigment is finely
ground—this ensures that the finished product isn't too grainy.
The mixture is added to hot wax and stirred for several hours until
it reaches the right consistency. Once a uniform consistency and

IT'S A FACT...

- According to a recent survey, 87 percent of American women admitted to leaving traces of lipstick in unwanted places.

- According to a recent survey, 65 percent of women wear lipstick; 25 percent of women won't even consider leaving the house without it!

- The expression "Putting lipstick on a pig" is used to describe a futile attempt to make something ugly superficially attractive.

- Pearlescence, a silvery substance found in fish scales, is added to lipstick to give a shimmering effect.

- In the 18th century lipstick became particularly popular with men especially in the French court circle where they would apply carmine mixed with grease to their lips to make them look colourful against beards and moustaches.

- The average lipstick factory produces more than 2,400 tubes of lipstick an hour.

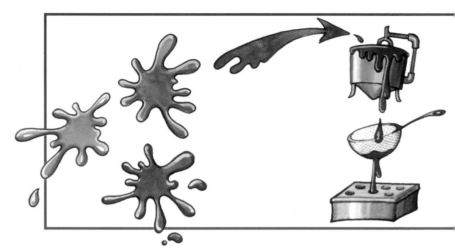

color have been achieved, the liquid is strained and sent to the molding station. The semi-hard lipstick mass is melted and then agitated in vats to remove any trapped air. The solution is poured into cold metal molds that consist of the bottom part of the dispensing tube and a shaping portion, and the molds are then cooled in refrigerators after which the solidified lipstick is removed. One end of the dispensing tube is sealed and the open end of the lipstick is passed through a flame for half a second—this gives a smooth, glossy finish and removes any imperfections.

The finished lipstick is then inspected for blemishes

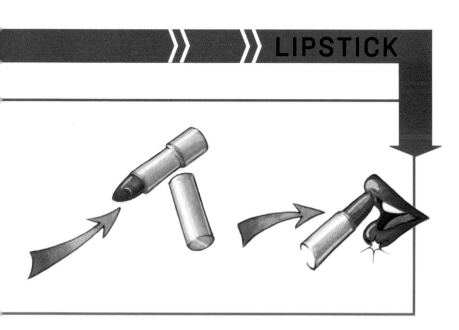

and air holes. Any reworking is carried out by hand using delicate spatulas. The tubes of lipstick are retracted and capped and sent off to the labeling and packaging area. Because lipstick is the only cosmetic that is ingested, hygiene throughout the process is vitally important. Strict Food and Drug Administration standards must be met. It makes you wonder what the FDA would have made of Cleopatra's outlandish production methods . . .

This sweet, spongy candy has been a popular confection in one form or another for more than two thousand years. In ancient Egypt, royalty used to mix the root of the bushy marshmallow plant with honey. The results became such a delicacy that marshmallow was considered food for the gods. The marshmallow is actually an herb that grows in marshy areas—hence the name. It has pretty pale pink flowers and a fleshy stem that contains medicinal qualities such as an effective laxative and a cure for sore throats, coughs, and chest pains! Marshmallow as we know it today began in France back in the 1850s; however, the production method was prohibitively expensive and painfully slow, since each marshmallow had to be molded individually by hand. As a result, only the upper classes could afford to buy the confection.

It would be another fifty years before marshmallow became the popular mass-produced sweet we know and love today. By the mid-1950s, there were more than thirty marshmallow manufacturers in the United States, due in part to Alex Doumak of Doumak, Inc. Doumak invented the revolutionary *extrusion process,* which is still used by modern manufacturers. There are three main marshmallow manufacturers left in the United States, but between them, they produce an awful lot of the fluffy stuff.

Marshmallow certainly isn't the healthiest food in the world, the two main ingredients being sweeteners and emulsifiers. The manufacturing process is pretty straightforward and involves combining sugar with corn syrup and dissolving the mixture in boiling water to form a gooey brew. Egg whites and gelatin (which is extracted from the hooves of barnyard animals) are added and then boiled at 240 degrees Fahrenheit in a special kettle. The hot mixture is passed through a sieve to remove lumps and then beaten into a

MARSHMALLOW

foam that bulks to more than three times its original volume. Flavorings are added to the mixture, which is then sent to a heat exchanger, where air is pumped into the marshmallow mix.

Older recipes used to contain the mucilaginous root of the marshmallow plant, but that has since been replaced with gelatin. Now that you know where gelatin comes from, will you still be tempted to ask for "s'more" next time someone offers you a melted marshmallow between chocolate and two graham crackers?

Creating fire hasn't always been as simple as striking a match. Anyone who has ever been camping will know the difficulty and frustration of trying to strike two rocks together to form a spark that may or may not lead to fire.

The earliest form of the match is said to date back to 577 CE when Chinese women dipped pinewood sticks into sulfur to create fires for cooking. How they actually achieved this remains a bit of a mystery.

An Englishman named John Walker invented the first friction match back in 1827 by mixing gum, potassium chlorate, antimony sulphide, and starch together. Back then there were no matchboxes, so instead Walker's matches were ignited by pulling them through a fold of paper coated in ground-up glass. The method was clumsy and the matches were notoriously hard to light. They also gave off an overpoweringly noxious odor. By 1831 the process had been refined somewhat by a Frenchman named Charles Sauria who created the first match made of white phosphorous. Unlike Walker's invention, Sauria's matches flared up into a dangerously volatile flame that became a real fire hazard. For safety, Sauria's were the first matches to be kept in a box. Apart from the unpredictable flame, phosphorous matches also had a devastating effect on the factory workers who produced them. Inhaling the toxic fumes led to "phosphorus necrosis of the jaw" or "phossy jaw," a particularly gruesome illness that affected the sufferer's jawbone. After a while, the bone would literally start to glow green and then rot away completely. This in turn led to terminal brain damage and a slow, painful death. Removal of the jawbone was the only known cure, but it left the patient quite literally speechless.

In addition to all these problems, the invention of matches led to a huge increase in smoking.

So how are these little beacons of light made? Well, matches begin life in the vast pine forests of Scandinavia. Pine is ideal for making matches, because it is porous enough to absorb chemicals yet strong enough to withstand the rigors of repeated striking. Pine is also straight-grained, making it easier to cut into smaller sticks. Once the logs arrive at the factory, they are placed in rotating debarking machines where spinning blades remove all the outer bark. The logs are then cut into approximately two-foot lengths and placed onto rotating peelers that cut thin sheets or veneers from the surface until all that's left is a *core post* that is either discarded or recycled into paper. The veneers, which are only about 3 millimeters thick, are stacked in piles before being fed into chopping machines that cut each veneer down to match-size proportions. The tiny sticks are then tossed in ammonium phosphate, which acts as a fire retardant to prevent the finished matches from smoldering once they've been blown out. Our little wooden friends are then transferred to a large rotating drying machine. The tumbling

motion also polishes the matches and removes any loose debris and splinters. The dry sticks are dropped into a hopper, where a powerful machine blows them directly onto a perforated steel belt. The sticks are then dumped into V-shaped hoppers that drop them into the holes of another perforated belt. A series of plungers push the matches securely into place. They are then suspended upside down from the perforated belt. The matchstick tips pass through a river of hot paraffin wax that soaks into the stems about a third of the way up (the wax slows down the burn speed of the ignited chemicals, keeping the flame alight for longer). The matches are then dried in an oven for fifteen seconds before being moved to the match-head chemical zone. Match heads contain four fillers, sulphur to fuel the flame, gelatin and silica to bind the chemicals to the matchstick, and potassium chlorate for oxidation. Powdered glass may also be added to increase the friction needed for light-ing. Animal glue binds everything together. The chemicals are then mixed together with hot water to form a slushy batter. The match-

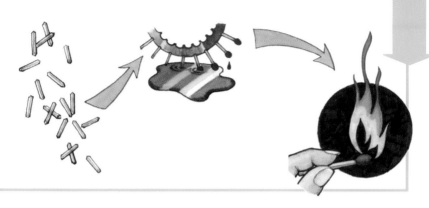

stick tips pass through the batter, picking up just the right amount to form a head. An average batch of chemical batter can make more than twenty-five million match heads.

The matches are then left to dry for about an hour. Meanwhile, in another part of the factory, the matchboxes are being prepared. Large sheets of cardboard are cut down to size and folded into either inner boxes or outer sleeves. The brand logo is printed on the front of each outer sleeve. The dried matches move along a conveyor belt until they reach a large pronged wheel that pushes them through holes in the belt. The matches drop into hoppers that filter them directly into the inner boxes. Running alongside is another conveyor belt containing the outer sleeves. Both belts stop momentarily as the inner boxes are pushed into the outer sleeves. A small strip of sandpaper needed for striking is glued to the side of each box (for safety matches, the igniting chemicals are mixed in with the sandpaper so they can only be lit from the actual matchbox). So now these little miracles are ready to burn, baby, burn!

If it weren't for water, there wouldn't be mirrors. Early hunters first caught sight of their reflection in pools and lakes while out looking for fish. And so man's love affair with his reflection began. Those early hunters soon discovered that certain stones such as obsidian, a naturally occurring volcanic glass, also reflected light and could therefore be used as mirrors. So rather than having to trudge down to the lake whenever they wanted to check their hair, they could instead carry their reflection about with them.

The first man-made mirrors were little more than polished sheets of metal that gave a wobbly, distorted reflection. By coating glass with a mixture of tin and mercury, European manufacturers created a less distorted reflection. During the sixteenth century, Venice became a center for mirror production using this revolutionary technique. Glass mirrors were such an expensive luxury that only the upper classes could afford them.

In 1835, a German chemist named Justus von Liebig invented the first silver-backed mirror, the sort we still use today. But mirrors don't simply feed our vanity—they are a vital component in many scientific instruments such as telescopes, lasers, and microscopes, and are also used in high-definition TVs and cameras.

Glass makes the ideal base material for mirrors because it has an even surface with very few distortions. But because glass only reflects about 4 percent of light, it needs to have a coating of bright reflective metal on the back in order to turn it into a mirror.

Robotic arms lay glass panels onto a conveyor belt, which transports them to a washing station. Sprayers blast the glass with water and powdered soil called *syrium oxide*. Rotating brushes scrub and polish both sides of the glass to remove any scuff marks. The glass is then sprayed with hot demineralized water (the miner-

IT'S A FACT...

- Early examples of obsidian mirrors have been found in Anatolia (now called Turkey). These date back to around 6000 BCE. Polished stone mirrors from Central and South America date from around 2000 BCE onward.

- Metal-coated mirrors were first invented in Lebanon back in the first century CE.

- A mirror is defined as an object with a "good specular reflection." This means it has a smooth enough surface to form a perfectly reflected image.

- Mirrors used to be called "looking glasses."

- Unlike a normal mirror, two-way mirrors only reflect some of the light, allowing the rest to pass through. This is achieved by coating the glass with an incredibly thin layer of metal only a few atoms thick. Two-way mirrors only work when used between a dark and a brightly lit room. On the brightly lit side you can only see your own reflection, whereas on the darker side you can see through to the bright side.

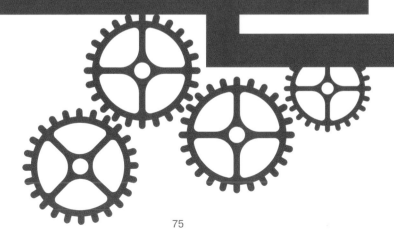

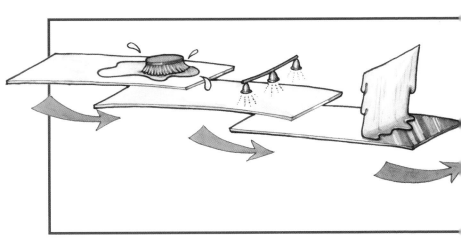

als in normal water may damage the reflective materials that come later).

A layer of liquefied tin is applied to one side of the glass panel. This will become the back of the mirror. An incredibly fine mist of liquid silver (some manufacturers prefer aluminum) mixed with a chemical activator is then sprayed over the tin. As soon as the silver hits the tin, it hardens to form a perfect reflecting surface. To preserve and protect the delicate silver backing, a machine sprays on a layer of hard protective copper. The mirror then passes through a dryer at 160 degrees Fahrenheit. Any moisture left on the surface quickly evaporates. The

IT'S A FACT...

In the famous Greek legend, Narcissus fell in love with his own reflection.

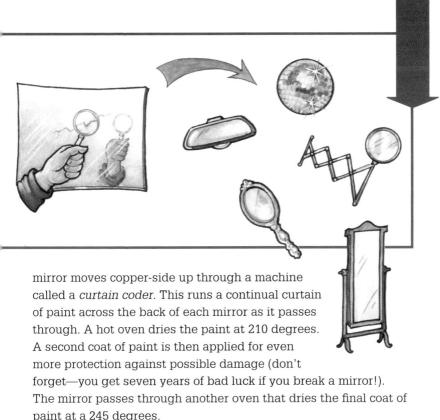

mirror moves copper-side up through a machine called a *curtain coder*. This runs a continual curtain of paint across the back of each mirror as it passes through. A hot oven dries the paint at 210 degrees. A second coat of paint is then applied for even more protection against possible damage (don't forget—you get seven years of bad luck if you break a mirror!). The mirror passes through another oven that dries the final coat of paint at a 245 degrees.

The shiny new mirror is removed from the conveyor belt and held vertically, ready for a visual inspection. Any faults, such as bubbles or scratches, are removed by cutting away that particular section of mirror. The completed mirror is now ready to be admired, along with the reflection within. Well, it beats having to go down to the lake every time you want to brush your hair . . .

This clever little device has been holding two or more pieces of paper together for nearly a hundred and fifty years. Samuel B. Fay, who patented the first paper clip, designed them mainly to hold labels on garments. It was Erlman J. Wright who patented the first device exclusively designed to hold sheets of paper together. The iconic oval *gem* paper clip was never actually patented, although the Gem Manufacturing Company began production toward the end of the nineteenth century. The gem is still the most widely used clip.

The manufacturing process, although simple, has remained unchanged since the early twentieth century. Paper clips originate underground! The steel from which paper clips are made comes from a combination of basic elements found in the earth such as iron ore, chromium, silicon, nickel, carbon, nitrogen, and manganese. For a paper clip to be effective, the science has to be just right. The wire needs to be malleable enough to bend, but strong enough not to break or lose its gripping tension. The steel therefore needs to be galvanized. This involves passing the steel through a bath of molten zinc at a temperature of around 870 degrees Fahrenheit. When exposed to the atmosphere, the thin coating of zinc reacts with oxygen to form zinc oxide, which then reacts with carbon dioxide to form zinc carbonate—a strong material that protects the steel and stops it from being corroded by the elements. You can tell galvanized steel by the crystallization patterning on the surface known as a *spangle*.

Enormous spools of galvanized steel wire are transported to the paper clip factory. A paper clip is essentially made up of three bends. But before the bending process can begin, the wire must be cut up into four-inch lengths (the length of an unfurled paper clip) and then fed into a special wire-bending machine. The wire passes through a series of small wheels. The first bends the wire 180 degrees, the other two complete the classic three-bends shape. The process happens at such lightning speed that the machine can churn out literally hundreds of clips a minute. The completed paper clips are dropped into boxes and shipped.

Pasta, that most traditional of Italian dishes, was actually invented in China. In 1225, explorer Marco Polo returned to Venice from his exploits in the Far East armed with a cargo of Chinese noodles. So popular was his exotic find that by the fifteenth century the newly named *pasta* had become a staple of Italian cooking. Manufacturing began in Naples, which to this day remains a major producer.

Pasta is made from two main ingredients—semolina and water. Semolina is a powdery substance that comes from dried durum wheat, a hard variant of traditional wheat grown in vast fields all across Italy. When it arrives at the pasta factory, the semolina is stored in giant silos that can carry up to thirty-three tons. The semolina is then transported to a pre-mixer where it is vigorously blended with water for about ten seconds. These pre-mixing machines can treat up to two tons of semolina per hour. The thickened dough is removed and transferred to an open mixer and then on to a vacuum mixer that continues to churn the dough using revolving blades. The mixture is now ready to be passed through intricate brass molds that contain all the many different shapes of pasta from good old spaghetti (which comes from the diminutive for the Italian word for "thread") to the more exotic strozzapreti (which means "priest stranglers"). A heavy press forces the thick dough through the mold. A revolving blade situated just underneath the mold cuts the pasta into correct lengths as it oozes through. In the case of lasagna, strips of pasta 107 inches long are hung vertically from poles and left to dry for fifteen hours at 149 degrees Fahrenheit. Scissors then cut the lasagna noodles into standard 10-inch strips, which are left out to dry. Spaghetti is also dried vertically in long reams before being laid flat and cut into long or short varieties.

PASTA

IT'S A FACT...

▸ A typical pasta factory can produce up to a hundred different types of pasta product using as much as 396 tons of semolina a day.

▸ Pasta noodles are traditionally ten inches long.

▸ There are said to be over a thousand different pasta shapes on the market, although because new ones are being invented all the time, that figure is continually rising!

Short pastas such as bows and macaroni need to be dried, too, so once they've passed through the molds, they are placed in huge drying machines. When the shapes eventually emerge, they are hard and ready to be packaged. A computer determines the amount of pasta per packet before sending the specified amount down a zigzag-shaped chute. Another chute lines up the pasta and drops just the right amount into pre-positioned bags. The amazing bagging machine can fill ten nine-pound bags of spaghetti in just under a minute. For smaller amounts, it can fill up to sixty bags per minute.

Now all you need is a delicious sauce to go with all that amaz-

ing pasta—but remember, Italians are extremely particular about which sauce goes with which pasta: Thin, delicate pastas such

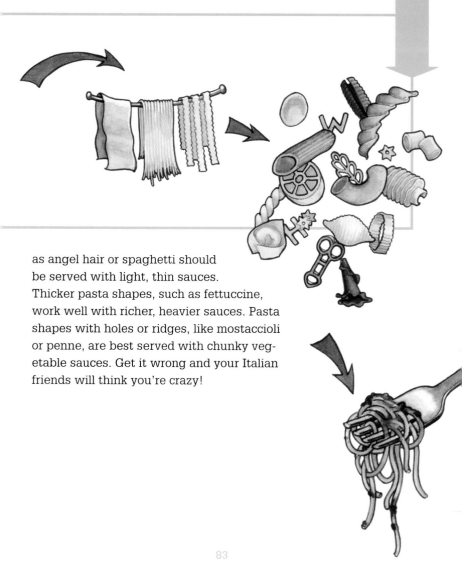

as angel hair or spaghetti should
be served with light, thin sauces.
Thicker pasta shapes, such as fettuccine,
work well with richer, heavier sauces. Pasta
shapes with holes or ridges, like mostaccioli
or penne, are best served with chunky vegetable sauces. Get it wrong and your Italian
friends will think you're crazy!

Pity the poor peanut as it journeys from the vast agricultural plains of rural Georgia to the grocery store shelf. En route, this tasty little nut will be pulled up, broken down, crushed, packaged, and finally eaten.

The United States is the third-largest producer of peanuts in the world after India and China, but the peanuts it produces are considered the best for peanut butter. Most other countries crush their peanuts to use as oil.

Peanut bushes are planted after the last frosts in late April when soil temperatures reach sixty-five to seventy degrees Fahrenheit. Surprisingly, peanuts aren't officially classified as nuts—botanically speaking they are part of the legume or vegetable family. Four types of peanut are grown in the United States: Runner, Virginia, Spanish, and Valencia. Thousands of farmers and their families representing fifteen states plant, nurture, and harvest these peanuts.

Let's follow the journey of a typical peanut from Georgia. We'll call him George. The farm where young George grew up is more than a hundred acres in size and as flat as a sheet. Peanut kernels from the previous year's crop are planted two inches under the soil, approximately two inches apart in long rows. Pre-planting tillage ensures a rich, well-prepared seedbed for George to feed on. Peanut seedlings crack the soil about ten days after planting and grow into a green, oval-leafed plant about eighteen inches tall. Unlike most plants, the peanut flowers above ground, but yields fruits below ground. Yellow flowers appear about forty days after planting. Once the flowers pollinate themselves, the petals fall off as the peanut ovary containing young George begins to form. This budding ovary, called a *peg* grows away from the plant on a vine.

When the plant reaches full maturity, it produces about forty

IT'S A FACT...

▸ The average U.S. household consumes about six pounds of peanut butter every year. That's more than 570 million pounds . . . enough to cover the floor of the Grand Canyon.

▸ "Arachibutyrophobia" (pronounced I-RA-KID-BU-TI-RO-PHO-BI-A) is the fear of peanut butter sticking to the roof of your mouth.

▸ The average American child will eat 1,500 peanut butter sandwiches by the time he or she graduates from high school.

▸ Peanuts contribute more than four billion dollars to the U.S. economy each year. Americans spend almost eight hundred million dollars a year on peanut butter. That's a lot of Georges!

▸ It is claimed that renowned agriculturalist, peanut expert, and equal rights campaigner George Washington Carver invented more than 300 different uses for the peanut.

pods that then grow into the familiar peanut-shaped shells. Shells have two chambers, each containing a fully grown peanut.

Peanut farmers tend to follow a three-year rotation pattern with cotton, corn, or grass crops. Peanut plants need two inches of water per week during kernel development. If rain doesn't meet those needs, farmers will have to irrigate the fields. Without adequate rainfall, non-irrigated peanuts begin to show drought stress.

Peanuts are typically harvested 120 to 160 days after planting. The harvesting process occurs in two stages. When more than 70 percent of the crop has reached maturity, a *digger-inverter* loosens

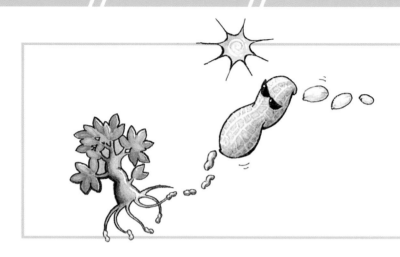

the plant and severs the taproot with a horizontal blade running about four inches below the soil surface. The *digger-shaker* lifts the plant from the ground, gently shakes the soil from the peanuts, and lays the plant upside down to cure in the sun for two or three days.

When the peanuts are dry, a harvester separates them from the vines, placing the peanuts into a hopper on the top of the machine and depositing the vines back in the field. Freshly dug peanuts are then placed into peanut wagons for further curing with forced warm air circulating through the wagon. In this final stage, the moisture content is reduced to 10 percent for storage.

Once peanuts have been harvested and cured, they are called "farmer stock peanuts" (harvested peanuts that have not been shelled, cleaned, or crushed) and are inspected and graded while still in the shell to establish their quality and value. Several samples from each peanut wagon must be taken and inspected before they can be sold. U.S. peanuts must be certified as safe for consumption. Peanuts certified as wholesome (more than 99 percent

PEANUT BUTTER

of the U.S. crop last year) are graded by size and type according to industry standards.

Once graded, George will move on to the shelling process where he is cleaned of soil, bits of vine, and other materials. He'll then move along a conveyor belt where shelling machines remove his kernel. The kernels pass over various screens where they are sorted by size into market grades.

The edible George is individually inspected with electronic eyes, video cameras, and laser sorters. Discolored or defective kernels are removed and destroyed. Once the peanuts have been shelled, they are packed into boxes and then onto railcars for delivery to the peanut butter plant. Each railroad car holds approximately 190,000 pounds of peanuts (about the weight of sixteen elephants!). After the nuts have been crushed, they are mixed with oil, brown sugar, and salt and then packaged and sent out to supermarkets around the world.

When a friend of multimillionaire John Paul Getty asked what he should buy for the man who had everything, Getty replied, "How about a really good lead pencil?" While it's certainly true that a good pencil is a wonder to behold, it's actually a myth that they contain lead.

Back in 1665, a bunch of prospectors found a huge graphite deposit in the hills outside Borrowdale in northern England and mistook the metallic black substance for lead. It would be several years before anyone realized their mistake, by which time the name "lead pencil" had already stuck. Even today, people often mistakenly refer to the graphite in pencils as lead. What these early pioneers had discovered was in fact the perfect drawing tool, which is why they started mining the stuff and then whittling the pure slivers of graphite into useable pencils. To keep the brittle graphite sticks from breaking during use, they were wrapped in twine. Word spread throughout the art world, and the pencil soon became an indispensible tool for artists and jotters everywhere.

By the late eighteenth century, the mine at Borrowdale was running low on graphite. Although small deposits were being mined elsewhere in the world, the graphite never seemed to be as pure as that original find in Borrowdale. In order to remove impurities, the graphite had to be crushed down to dust. It was a French chemist named Nicolas-Jacques Conté who discovered that if you mixed graphite dust with water and powdered clay, you could mold and bake the mixture to form a writing implement every bit as good as pure graphite. His methods live on today.

Pencils come in twenty different levels of hardness—the more graphite used in the mixture, the harder the pencil and the lighter the line. Batches of the various clay/graphite mixtures are forced through narrow molds to form a long, thin, snakelike string of

IT'S A FACT...

▸ The word "pencil" comes from the Latin *pencillus*, meaning "little tail," and "graphite" comes from the Latin *graphein*, meaning "to write."

▸ Pencils are hexagonal in shape for a very good reason—to stop them from rolling off the desk!

▸ There is a pencil museum in Keswick, England, near where the first graphite deposits were found.

▸ American Harry W. Lipman came up with the bright idea of attaching erasers to the ends of pencils.

▸ In 1812 the first pencil factory was set up in the United States.

▸ Graphite is one of the only three forms of pure carbon. The other two are coal and diamonds.

graphite that is then cut into pencil lengths and dried in large ovens. These hardened cores move along a conveyor belt and into a holder.

Meanwhile, in northern California, incense cedar trees are being felled and chopped, ready to be transported to our pencil factory. Cedar is particularly good for pencils because it can sustain repeated sharpening without splintering. (And it smells great, too!)

When the wood blocks arrive at the factory, they have usually been dried, stained, and waxed to prevent them from warping. The logs are sawed into flat, narrow, oblong sheets called *slats* that are about seven inches long, half an inch thick, and two and a half inches wide. The slats are put into a feeder and then dropped onto a conveyor belt before being planed to create a good flat surface.

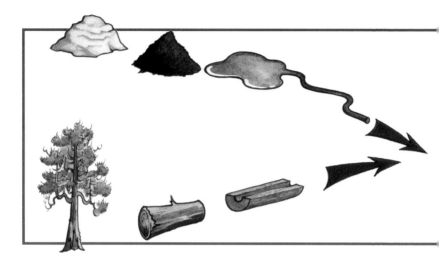

A cutter carves out a semicircular groove big enough to accommodate the graphite core down the length of each slat. As they pass along the conveyor belt, half the slats receive a coating of glue. The lengths of graphite are then dropped into the sticky grooves. The empty, glue-free slats are removed and placed on another conveyor belt upside down with the groove facing downward. Both conveyor belts converge with the two slats being placed on top of each other to form a sandwich with the graphite stick as the filling. Metal clamps squeeze and hold the two sides together with the aid of a powerful hydraulic press. When the graphite sandwiches have dried, the gluey ends are trimmed. The slats are now ready to be turned into proper pencils. To make the hexagonal pencil we all know and love, two sets of cutters positioned above and below the slats cut out the familiar shape—each length of sandwich produces between six and nine pencils.

But the pencil's journey from forest to desk isn't finished yet. It

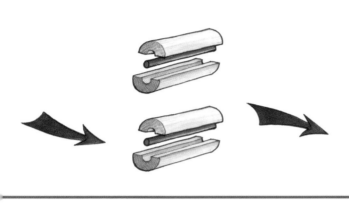

now needs to be sanded and dipped several times into vats of varnish or color. Felt buffers remove any excess varnish and the shiny new pencils are sent on another journey along a conveyor belt through a shaping machine that cuts the ends of the pencils to make sure they are all the same length. If erasers are to be added, they are held in place by *ferrules*, which are metal casings glued to one end of the pencil. The company logo and hardness indicator are etched into the finished pencil using a heated steel die. The brightly colored scribblers are boxed and shipped to art and office supply stores around the world.

And it all began in a small mine in northern England.

Since the dawn of time, humans have been trying to mask their natural body odor with sweet-smelling scents and animal secretions. Early Egyptians (them again) used to soak wood and resins in water and oil and use the liquid as a fragrant body lotion. The art of perfume-making, or "perfumery," started in ancient Mesopotamia and Egypt but it was the Romans and Persians who developed and refined the process. Archaeologists recently discovered what are believed to be the oldest perfumes in the world. The scents, found in Cyprus, are more than four thousand years old and were discovered in an ancient perfume factory containing distilling apparatuses, mixing bowls, funnels, and perfume bottles. The original factory itself was huge, totaling more than forty-three thousand square feet.

Back then, people much preferred the smell of herbs and spices such as almond, coriander, and myrtle to the flowery scents we use today. A Persian chemist by the name of Avicenna first introduced the process of making perfume that is still most commonly used—that of extracting oils from flowers by means of distillation.

The manufacturing process begins with the gathering of raw materials such as hand-picked flowers, fatty substances from animals, and synthetic aromatic chemicals. To extract the oils from plants, flower petals are distilled using a steaming method that heats up the essential oils until they turn to gas. The gas is then cooled in tubes until it liquefies (an alternative extraction method known as *expression* involves manually pressing flowers or citrus fruit until the oil is squeezed out).

Certain animal scents have primeval qualities that we find irresistible, which is why they are used in perfume. The most intoxicating scents are: musk (from the glands of the Asian musk

IT'S A FACT...

▶ It can take more than nine hundred different ingredients and many years of development before a "nose" is satisfied with his odorous creation.

▶ The prophet Mohammed claimed that perfumes were "foods that awaken the spirits."

▶ It takes thousands of flowers to produce just one pound of perfume oil.

▶ The word "perfume" comes from the Latin *per fumum,* meaning "through smoke."

deer and Civet cat), ambergris (a fatty compound expelled by sperm whales but unavailable since the whaling ban of 1977), and castoreum (extracted from the anal glands of the North American beaver). Because many of the animals used in perfumery are on the endangered list, musk is becoming increasingly difficult to source and is commonly replaced by synthetic substitutes.

Once the musk has been collected, it is mixed with essential oils and blended into a formula by a perfume expert known as a *nose.* When the final scent has been decided upon, it is diluted in varying amounts of alcohol and water. The strongest perfumes contain about 20 percent pure perfume oil, whereas eau de cologne may only contain 2 percent.

The finest and most expensive perfumes can be left to mature for several years. At the end of the aging process, the nose will decide whether the perfume has reached the desired pungency by testing the three essential *notes*—top (the first and shortest lasting

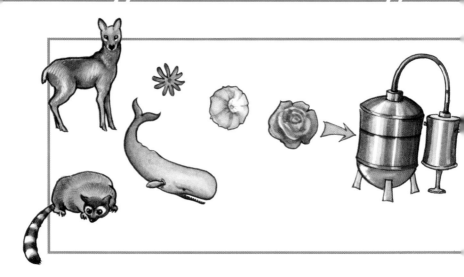

scent), middle, and base (the longest lasting scent, which can take hours to form).

Finished perfumes come in several different categories, including:

Soliflore: the scent of a single flower

Floral Bouquet: the perfume of several flowers

Woody: foresty aromas such as cedar and sandalwood

Oriental: a combination of amber, vanilla, and animal scents, along with flowers and woods

Musk: animal- or vegetable-based scents

Leather: hints of tobacco, wood, and wood tars, as well as a scent that alludes to leather

Fougere: (Fern in French) lavender, coumarin, and oakmoss— woody scents often found in men's fragrances

Chypre: (Cyprus in French) fragrances of bergamont, oakmoss, and labdanum

Oceanic/Ozone: a clear, androgynous scent

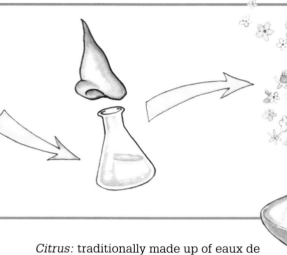

Citrus: traditionally made up of eaux de cologne with a lemon or other citrus fruit fragrance

Fruity: berry or stone fruit, often with light musks or vanilla

Gourmand: sweet, dessertlike aromas such as vanilla, chocolate, and caramel

Rumor has it that the original potato chip was invented by a chef named George Crum who worked at a restaurant near Saratoga Springs, New York. On August 24, 1853, he apparently lost his cool when a customer sent back his fried potatoes, claiming they were too thin and soggy. Exasperated, Crum cut the potatoes so thin they couldn't even be picked up with a fork. He then stir fried them to a hard, curly crisp. Much to Crum's surprise, his troublesome customer was delighted with the new potato "chips," and so it was that the "Saratoga chip" became a popular addition to the restaurant's menu. Word soon spread throughout New York and New England. Chips have subsequently gone on to become one of the most popular snack foods on the planet.

It's important that chips are made with freshly harvested potatoes that are fewer than twenty-four hours old (fresh potatoes are less blackened and bruised). After a brushing machine has removed all the dirt and debris, the potatoes are sent along a fast-moving water canal and into a revolving peeling machine. While in the machine, the potatoes tumble against abrasive rollers that gradually remove the skin. The jacketless spuds then travel along a filtering machine that separates them by size.

The potatoes are now sent to a revolving slicer that can be set at different thicknesses and shapes. The centrifugal force inside the spinning drum pushes the potatoes up against sharp blades set into the walls. Regular chips are cut to six one hundredths of an inch in thickness. Now that's thin! The slices are then fed into a giant revolving drum, where they are washed in cold water for about a minute. The slices then pass under a hot-air blower to dry off any excess water.

Now comes the most important part of the process: The slices

POTATO CHIP

IT'S A FACT...

- Automated potato peelers peel more than twelve thousand pounds of potatoes an hour!

- It takes just fifteen minutes to turn a raw potato into a bag of chips!

- An average potato contains about thirty-six chips.

- Because potatoes are 80 percent water, it takes almost four pounds of potatoes to make one pound of potato chips.

- A whopping 1.2 billion pounds of potato chips are devoured in the US every year.

- March 14th is National Potato Chip Day.

- Pennsylvania is said to produce the best potatoes for chip making due to the richness of the local soil.

- The average American eats 140 pounds of potatoes every year.

are dropped into a vat of boiling oil. Three minutes later the pale potato slices have been transformed into delicious golden chips. As they exit the fryer, any excess oil drips away through the conveyor belt. The chips are then covered in a generous sprinkling of salt before being sent to the sorter, where a special camera checks for black spots and defects. If any defective chips are found, the camera sends a message to one of several thin pipes hanging above the sorter. The pipe then blows the defective chip off the belt with a blast of high-pressure air.

Some chips that make it through are then placed in another large revolving drum and tossed in powdered flavor-

ing, such as cheese, sour cream and onion, or barbecue. A star-shaped machine then weighs and portions the chips ready for packaging. Each portion of chips is dropped into a bag and heat-sealed.

Chef Crum would be impressed!

If all the oceans suddenly dried up tomorrow, they'd leave enough salt to cover the whole of North America in a layer nearly two miles deep! The world is literally packed full of salt. It's everywhere. Nearly everything we eat contains salt, even candy bars and ice cream. It's a sad irony that although our bodies need salt to survive, too much of the stuff can kill us.

Only 5 percent of the salt produced in the United States actually goes into food. More than 70 percent is used by chemical industries as a source of chlorine. Surprisingly, most of the table salt we use doesn't actually come from the ocean, but from salt mines buried deep underground. The mines contain evaporated salt deposits from ancient oceans that dried up millions of years ago. Giant salt veins are found all over the world, but extracting this valuable foodstuff is a dangerous business involving massive drills and high explosives. Sometimes pressure from inside the earth forces the salt deposits to the surface, forming great domes—many of these can be found along the Gulf Coast between Louisiana and Texas. The vast majority of salt, however, is found deep in the earth's crust.

Nowadays we tend to take salt for granted—it's cheap and readily available. But for primitive man, obtaining his recommended daily allowance meant consuming large amounts of meat, milk, and even seaweed (a good source of natural salt). Over time, as the population increased, humans began eating less meat, so it became necessary to obtain salt from other sources.

Underground salt deposits were often discovered accidentally by prospectors searching for oil. There are two ways of drilling for salt. In the first method, a large diamond-tipped drill takes core samples from an area known to contain deposits. These are then analyzed by scientists to check whether they are commercially viable. Once a suitably large deposit has been found, shafts are

IT'S A FACT...

- Salt has hundreds of different uses, from processing leather and food to water purification. Salt keeps roads clear during winter by melting snow and ice on contact. It is used in the preservation of hay and in meat packing. Sodium chloride is also a vital component in road building and in the refining of metal. Best of all, it helps freeze ice cream!

- The salt you sprinkle on your fries is possibly millions of years old!

- To extract salt from surface water, shallow pools are left to dry in the sun. "Solar salt," as it is known, is mainly used in chemicals. Each gallon of saline water produces about half a pound of salt.

- The recommended daily allowance of salt for adults is less than half an ounce per day.

- The salt used in food processing needs to be 99.99 percent pure sodium chloride to avoid ruining the taste and texture of food. Pure sodium chloride can keep canned food "fresh" for several years.

sunk deep down into the center of the deposit. In a process known as *undercutting*, a huge, chainsaw-like machine cuts down into the floor of the salt veins. Several large holes are drilled into the under-cut salt. These are then filled with dynamite or ammonium nitrate. The explosives are detonated from the surface using blasting caps attached to wires. Through careful positioning, the explosives cause salt pillars to form in a process known as *room and pillar*. These tightly packed pillars of salt keep the roof of the newly

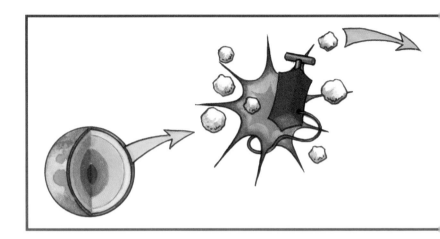

formed mine from collapsing. Hunks of blasted rock salt are then taken to an underground crusher consisting of large rotating cylinders with vicious jaws and spiked teeth. The chunks of crushed salt are then brought to the surface in elevators and transported to another crushing machine that breaks the chunks down to smaller nuggets.

In a cleaning process known as *picking*, the salt is placed in an enormous revolving drum called a Bradford Breaker. The drum is full of holes that allow the salt chunks to filter through as it tumbles. Hard rocks and other underground debris remain trapped inside the drum. Magnets are used to remove any metal deposits. Smaller bits of detritus are removed by hand, which can often be a long and laborious process.

From here the clean salt is put through yet another crusher that produces rocks of salt about an inch in diameter. For fine table salt, the rocks are ground between two metal cylinders. The granules

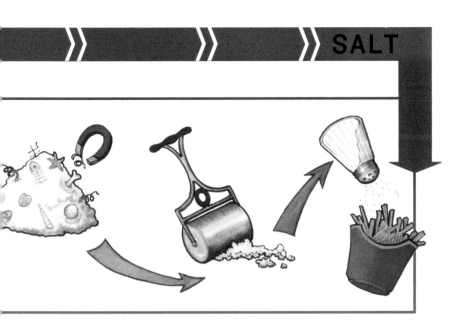

are sifted into different-sized batches and tested for solubility (a .71-ounce batch should take no more than twenty minutes to dissolve in seven ounces of water). After quality checks have been carried out, the salt is sent to packaging factories, where it is boxed or bagged and sent out to shops.

The hydraulic method of salt extraction involves drilling two large wells deep into the core of the salt beds. Fresh water is then pumped at very high pressure into one of the wells using a pipe. The salt dissolves on contact. The salty water, known as brine, is then forced to the surface through the second well. The brine is taken to refineries where the water is evaporated off leaving salt crystals, which are then placed in revolving cylinders. Hot air is pumped into the cylinders to quicken the drying process. The crystals are graded for grain size and purity before being packaged.

News just in: Silk comes from a worm's head!
Silk production, or *sericulture*, as it is known, can be traced
back several thousand years. The process was invented by the
Chinese and for generations remained a closely guarded secret.
Anyone suspected of divulging the formula could be executed.
Meanwhile, in the West, there was much speculation about how
this luxurious material was being produced. Pliny, the Roman
historian, thought he'd found the answer when he wrote in 70
BCE that "Silk is obtained by removing the down from leaves,
with the help of water . . ." How wrong he was!

Although many countries now manufacture the material,
China is still revered for the quality of its silk and is by far the
biggest producer.

Making silk is a process. The finest quality silks come from the
Bombyx mori moth, a blind, flightless creature whose only purpose
in life is to lay eggs that go on to hatch into highly prized silkworms. The average moth lays up to five hundred tiny eggs over
a four- or five-day period, after which it promptly dies. A typical
clutch of five hundred eggs weighs less than a quarter of an ounce.

Unlike the common wild moth that will eat virtually anything,
the mori feeds exclusively on mulberry leaves, which help its off-
spring produce a smooth, fine, uniform thread.

Although silkworms only live for about a month, an average
farm of thirty thousand worms will consume more than two thousand pounds of mulberry leaves in that time.

One of the reasons silk remains so expensive is because the
process is still so intricate and time-consuming. The tiny eggs have
to be kept in a temperature-controlled environment throughout the
incubation period. As soon as the worms hatch, they need to be
fed a diet of chopped mulberry leaves every half hour. The young

IT'S A FACT...

- There are many species of silk moth, but only the mori, mulberry, tasar, muga, and eri have any commercial value.

- It takes about thirty thousand worms to produce twelve pounds of silk.

- China still produces more than half of the world's silk.

- The male silkworm can smell a female silkworm from seven miles away.

- Silk is made of a tough elastic protein called fibroin.

worms are extremely sensitive to outside stimuli, so they have to be kept at a constant temperature and away from loud noises and strong smells such as fish and human sweat. If they are disturbed, they stop feeding. After a month of feasting on mulberry leaves, the worms have ballooned in size and are now strong enough to start spinning a cocoon. Two sacs on either side of the worm's body become engorged with a sticky liquid, which is secreted through a small opening next to the creature's mouth. On contact with the air, the liquid immediately hardens to form a protein-rich thread. The worm then hangs upside down from a tray and slowly begins to wind the thread around itself by swinging its head from side to side in a figure-eight motion. After about four days of continual winding, the cocoon is complete and resembles a soft, flossy ball with the worm safely hidden inside.

The cocoons are collected and kept in a warm place for eight days. They are then sent to the silk factory known as the *filature*. The cocoons are sorted according to color, size, shape, and texture (they come in a variety of colors, including white, yellow, and gray). Once they've been sorted, they are put through a series of hot and cold immersions. Hot steam kills the worms and softens the *sericin,* a gummy substance that holds the cocoon together. The cocoons are then placed in lukewarm water until they begin to unwind. In a laborious process known as *reeling*, a worker pushes a cocoon up and down in the water with a small brush until the end of the filament attaches itself to the bristles. The worker then gently unravels the incredibly delicate thread that can be up to four thousand yards long.

Individual filaments of silk are too fine for commercial use, so they need to be thickened. Workers weave up to ten filaments together to form a single strong thread known as *reeled silk*. The

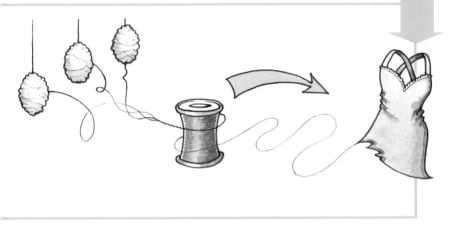

silk filament is reeled into skeins, which are then packed into small bundles called *books*. The books are transferred to bails that are shipped out to silk mills, where they are spun into luxuriously soft garments. Next time you run your fingers over a beautiful silk sheet, spare a thought for the talented silkworm.

You may not have realized it, but every time you wash your face with soap you could be rubbing animal fat into your skin! No wonder soap is perfumed! Back in 600 BCE the Phoenicians used to mix goat's tallow (fat) and wood ash together to form a primitive kind of soap. The Romans originally used soap for medicinal purposes. France, Italy, and Spain first used soap to remove dirt in the eighth century. Unfortunately, the rest of Europe didn't catch on until the seventeenth century. As a result, levels of cleanliness and hygiene in these areas remained low to smelly.

Soap comes in all sorts of shapes, textures, colors, and scents and is made from two basic ingredients—animal or vegetable fat and sodium hydroxide. Early soap makers used to simply boil up animal fat, mix it with wood ash, and then scrape off the foamy residue and allow it harden into a block. Eeew! Thankfully, these days animal fat used in soap doesn't come directly from the slaughterhouse. Soap makers tend to use fat known as fatty acids found in plants and animals, from which all the impurities have been removed.

The *cold process method* is the most common way to make soap. Fat and sodium hydrate are mixed together in a large vat. Water is then added to encourage a chemical reaction that transforms the fatty mess into a hot, soapy liquid. This liquid is sprayed onto a large metal roller, where it immediately solidifies before being cut into ribbons. These are mixed and compressed between two large steel rollers called *mills*. The compressed gloop is forced through a revolving die called a *noodle plate*. The minced soap is then dumped into a large mixer where powdered color and fragrant oils are added. The mixture is sent through a square *forming plate* that creates a long, continual block of soap that is cut down into regular-sized bars. A mechanical arm pushes them into a rotat-

IT'S A FACT...

▶ In the 1930s, soap companies used to sponsor fifteen-minute radio shows about ordinary people's lives. These were designed to grab the attention of the audience so that they would stick around for the commercial breaks in between programs. Thus, the soap opera was born!

▶ In the sixteenth century bathing was considered a luxury, which is why most people only bathed once a year. Couples tended to get married in June, just after they'd had their annual bath, which usually took place in May. However, by the time the big day arrived the happy couple was beginning to smell bad again. To mask the stench, the bride would carry a bouquet of flowers up the aisle. The tradition lives on, even though personal hygiene has (hopefully) improved since then!

ing die to shape them into ovals, circles, or squares. Mechanical presses move in and stamp each bar with the company logo, and suction pads fitted to a set of mechanical arms remove the slugs from the revolving die and drop them on a conveyor belt. The completed soap bars move through the wrapping station where a heated blade cuts and seals plastic wrapping around each bar. Grippers then slide the bars into waiting boxes.

The soap is now ready to do the job it was intended for, but how does this slimy, animal-based product actually get us

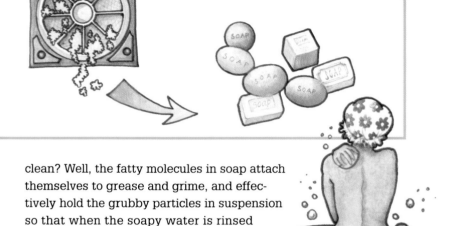

clean? Well, the fatty molecules in soap attach themselves to grease and grime, and effectively hold the grubby particles in suspension so that when the soapy water is rinsed away, the dirt is removed as well, leaving a clean and fragrant you!

Tennis balls were invented by Scottish craftsmen back in the sixteenth century, but unlike today's clean, aerodynamic design, these monstrosities were made of sheep stomach wrapped in wool and tied together with animal intestines and muscle tissue. Try winning Wimbledon with one of those! In England, tennis balls were slightly less yucky—mostly made of putty and covered with human hair. With the introduction of lawn tennis back in the 1870s, vulcanized rubber was used. This forms the basis of today's tennis balls.

Tennis balls start out as a continuous length of pure rubber mixed with fourteen to seventeen chemicals used to create the right consistency. The long strip is then cut down into little round nuggets. Each nugget will become one-half of a finished tennis ball. The nuggets are melted and compressed into a sheet of half-shell molds. The hardened half shells are then removed from the molds and sent to another part of the factory where they are fed into a revolving machine that shakes the concave shapes until they are all facing inside up. Another machine then coats the rims of the shells with glue that will eventually stick both sides of the finished ball together. A series of robotic arms containing suction pads removes several half-shells at a time and places them on a large rack. The shells are then manually placed onto a two-sided press that, when closed, brings both halves of the shell together to form a perfectly pressurized sphere. The dry, fully formed spheres, known as *cores*, are sent down a long shoot with abrasive edges that roughen up the rubber surfaces, preparing them for the next stage.

Factory workers then take two identically shaped pieces of felt material and apply them to each ball by hand. These unique shapes ensure a perfect, snug fit with no gaps or overlaps and no wastage. The felted balls then move along a conveyor belt that

TENNIS BALL

IT'S A FACT...

▸ Wilson, the world's biggest manufacturer of tennis balls, produces an average of four million balls a month—that's more than fifty million a year!

▸ More than three hundred million tennis balls are produced each year, contributing about sixty-four million dollars of waste in the form of rubber, most of which isn't biodegradable.

▸ According to the International Tennis Federation, all tennis balls must be either white or yellow.

▸ Most tennis balls are produced in Southeast Asia, where there is an abundance of rubber trees.

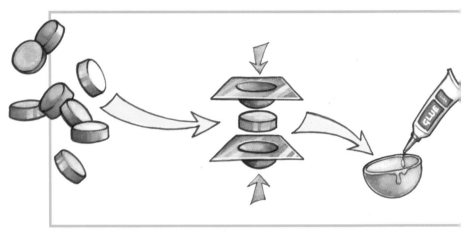

applies random pressure to ensure that the felt is fully adhered. The balls are cured in a press before being sucked along a chute to the logo printing area, where the name of the manufacturer is printed on each ball. Numbers are also printed on the balls so that players know which ones belong to them during court play. The balls are tested for bounce by being dropped from a height of a hundred inches onto concrete. In order to pass the bounce test, the ball must bounce up to between fifty-three and fifty-eight inches.

Three balls at a time are then dropped into plastic tube-shaped containers. The

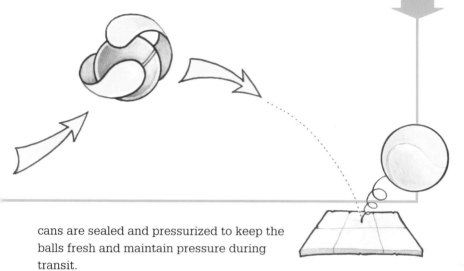

cans are sealed and pressurized to keep the balls fresh and maintain pressure during transit.

Match point!

Most of us take puppy-soft, quilted, moisturizer-enriched, air-infused toilet paper for granted. But consider the ancient Romans, who had to make do with a long, smooth, curvy stick made of wood or metal. If you were unlucky enough to need to use a public latrine back then, the best you could hope for was a dirty sponge or a stick in a bucket of salt water. In more arid climates, people used to clean their nether regions with soil or even sand (now that's got to hurt!). For many years, mussel shells and corncobs were popular, but all that changed when paper became widely available.

Although there are references to people using toilet paper as far back as sixth-century China, it wasn't until the fourteenth century that paper really caught on. In the Zhejiang Province alone, more than ten million packs of toilet paper were produced annually.

Bathroom tissue as we know it today is a relatively new invention dating to the end of the nineteenth century. The British Perforated Paper Company revolutionized personal hygiene with the invention of the first perforated toilet tissue euphemistically known as "Therapeutic Papers," which came in boxes rather than on rolls (the first tissue on a roll was introduced in 1890).

Although a lot of toilet paper is comprised of recycled material, much is still made from virgin paper that comes from a mixture of hard and softwood trees. Softwoods such as Southern pine and Douglas fir have extra-long, clingy fibers that give the finished paper its strength. Surprisingly, it is hardwood trees such as maple and oak (which have much shorter fibers) that give the paper its softness.

Trees are delivered directly to the toilet paper factory, where they are immediately debarked. The trees are then cut into wood chippings about an inch across. A typical batch of wood chips

IT'S A FACT...

▸ The ideal thickness for toilet paper is 0.005 to 0.006 inches.

▸ In 1393, during the Ming Dynasty, Emperor Hongwu's imperial family commissioned fifteen thousand sheets of extra-soft, perfumed toilet paper.

▸ French courtiers would often use lace, wool, or hemp for toilet paper. Peasants, meanwhile, had to make do with using their hands!

▸ During World War II people were encouraged to use newspaper instead of toilet paper to help with the war effort, although one toilet paper manufacturer had the phrase "wipe out Hitler" printed onto every sheet!

weighing in at about fifty tons is mixed with approximately ten thousand gallons of chemicals that help break down the wood. The gooey sludge is placed in a huge sixty-foot pressure cooker known as the *digester*. During the three-hour cooking process, most of the moisture (wood is about 50 percent water) evaporates, leaving around twenty-five tons of cellulose fibers and a binding substance called *lignin*. Of this, only about fifteen tons is usable pulp. The pulp is then thoroughly washed until all the lignin and chemicals have been removed. Revolving knives cut up the dry pulp, making it ready for bleaching—the details of this process are a closely guarded secret, although chemicals such as chlorine are no longer

used. The bleached pulp is washed again to produce paper stock. At this stage, the mixture is mainly water with only a small amount of actual fiber. The liquid is passed through a series of giant rollers that remove any remaining water. Eighteen-foot wide sheets of matted fiber produced at a rate of more than six thousand feet a minute pass through heated cylinders known as *Yankee Dryers*. It takes less than a second to turn the wet pulp into a dry, delicate paper four-thousandths of an inch thick. As it leaves the dryers, the paper is creped with a metal blade to make it extra soft. Creping also makes the paper more flexible. The finished paper is wound onto enormous five-ton spools at a rate of more than one mile a minute. Each spool can hold up to forty-seven miles of paper. A rolling machine embosses the paper with a pattern that not only looks good but also makes the paper thicker and more absorbent.

In another part of the factory, the inner rolls are being constructed using two lengths of cardboard both three inches wide.

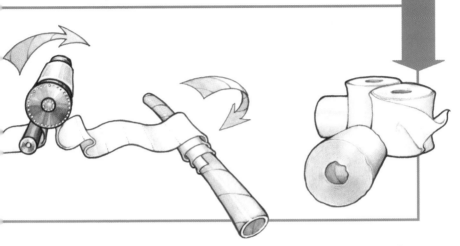

A machine coats the underside of one strip with glue, then winds the two strips diagonally to create a continuous cardboard tube. The long tubes are cut into sixty-five-inch lengths and transported by elevator to the toilet-paper area. Two huge spools of paper feed onto a winding machine, where the two sheets come together to form two-ply toilet paper. The paper is then rolled onto the long cardboard tubes. When a tube is full, it drops to make room for the next one. The machine then glues the ends of each roll of paper to prevent unraveling. A circular saw cuts each long roll down into sixteen standard-size rolls that are each four inches wide and now ready for packaging.

So there we have it—fluffy soft bathroom tissue. It beats wiping yourself with a corncob any day!

Next time you brush your teeth with refreshing, minty tooth-paste, remember that the ancient Chinese used ground-up fish bones to clean their teeth. Conditions weren't much better during the Middle Ages, when people used to scrub their teeth with sand and pumice stone. Here in the West, we used strong corrosive acids and table salt on our teeth. The first palatable toothpaste was invented in 1850 by a twenty-three-year-old dental surgeon named Washington Wentworth Sheffield. He called his new invention "crème dentrice," and it became so popular that he began his own highly successful manufacturing business in Connecticut.

Modern toothpastes have come a long way since the crushed fish bones of yore. Most now contain a cocktail of tooth-enhancing ingredients such as humectants, binders, soft abrasives, sudsers, flavors, sweeteners, preservatives, and water. Binders are used to thicken the paste and prevent the separation of the liquid and solid elements. Binders also affect the level of foam production and the rate at which flavoring is released, as well as how easily the paste is rinsed from the toothbrush. Abrasives such as chalk and silica are added to help remove plaque, but some of the harsher abrasives can actually end up damaging teeth. Sudsers give toothpaste its foaming quality by lowering water's surface tension so that thousands of tiny bubbles form. Foam is particularly good at getting at those hard-to-reach places between teeth.

Once all the raw materials have arrived at the factory, they are weighed and then mixed together in temperature-controlled vats that can typically produce enough toothpaste to fill ten thousand tubes. The plastic holding tubes pass under a high-powered blowing machine that removes any dust particles and detritus. The tubes are then sealed and capped at one end and opened up at the

TOOTHPASTE

IT'S A FACT...

▸ Peppermint is the most popular flavor of toothpaste, followed by spearmint, cinnamon, and wintergreen.

▸ Over a lifetime, the average American will spend a total of 38.5 days brushing his or her teeth.

▸ Prince Charles has a personal valet who puts toothpaste onto his toothbrush every morning.

▸ Fluoride was added to toothpaste in the mid-twentieth century.

▸ Americans spend more than two billion dollars a year on dental products.

▸ According to United States polls, Brad Pitt and Julia Roberts have the best-looking teeth in America.

other, ready to be filled. The tubes are moved to the filling station where an optical device rotates them to make sure they are properly aligned under the pump. Once the tubes have been filled with the right amount of paste, the other end is firmly sealed. Finally, the company logo is printed onto the side of each tube. They are then packed into open paperboard boxes and sent out to stores.

Don't forget to brush at least twice a day to keep the dentist at bay!

IT'S A FACT...

Toothpaste hasn't always come in tubes. It used to be packaged in jars.

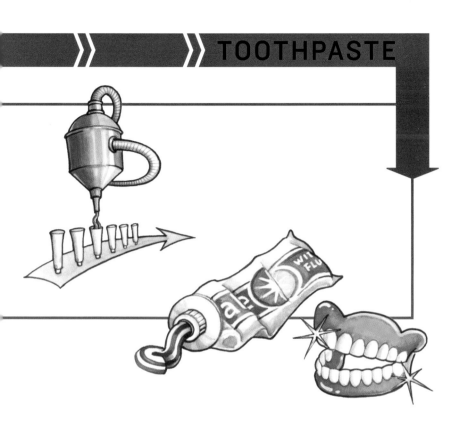

Poland and Russia both claim to have invented vodka. Although no one really knows for sure, vodka has certainly been around since the fourth century CE. But it wasn't until the 1950s that the drink became popular in the West. So how on earth do you turn solid foodstuff like wheat and potatoes into a clear, odorless alcoholic beverage? Well, it all begins with the harvest.

Although potatoes are still used in some cheaper brands, most vodka is now made from cereals. Rye is the main ingredient in most Polish vodkas, while wheat, oats, and barley make up Russian vodka. The factory or distillery either grows its own wheat or buys grain from outside sources. Once the grain has been harvested, it is loaded into large, revolving *mash tubs*. As the grain is turned, *agitators* break down the grain into mash. Malt meal is added to help convert the starch into sugar. At this stage it is important that the mixture is free from harmful bacteria, so the mash is boiled to aid sterilization. The mixture needs to ferment (the process in which sugar turns to alcohol), so the acidity level is raised by injecting the mash with lactic acid bacteria. Yeast is then added. After about four days, enzymes in the yeast convert the sugar to ethyl alcohol. The alcohol is pumped into tall steel columns called *stills* that contain a series of vaporizing chambers. As the liquor passes through the column, the alcohol is heated up with steam until it eventually vaporizes and condenses and all the impurities are removed. The vapor becomes concentrated in the upper chambers of the stills.

The leftover material in the lower chambers is sold off as animal feed, but the remaining concentrated vapor contains just under 100 percent pure alcohol or 190 proof. This would be lethal to drink, so water is added to bring it down to the standard 80 proof. The liquid is then sent to the bottling factory, where a highly mechanized process loads more than four hundred bottles a minute.

IT'S A FACT...

▸ Proof is the standard way of measuring alcohol content—each degree of proof is the equivalent of half a percent of alcohol.

▸ In some U.S. states it is illegal to produce home-made vodka.

▸ Every bottle of Bison Grass vodka contains a sprig of Polish grass that is said to have been peed on by a bison.

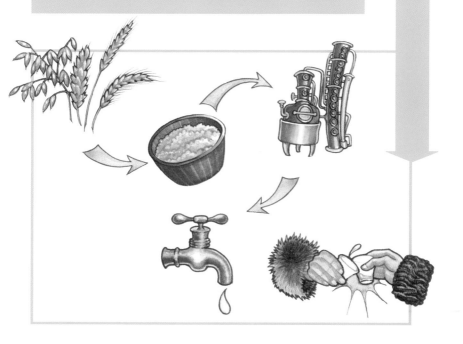

ACKNOWLEDGMENTS

Thanks to all the manufacturers who kindly assisted me in the compiling of this book. Thanks also to Wikipedia and enotes.

ABOUT THE AUTHOR

James Innes-Smith is the co-author of *Bad Hair* and the author of *Big Hair*. He has written and appeared in several films, TV shows, and theater productions. He has written for *The Daily Telegraph*, *What's On?*, and *Time Out* and divides his time between London and Los Angeles.

ABOUT THE ILLUSTRATOR

Henrietta Webb is the co-author of *Bad Hair*, as well as the illustrator of *Jane Austen's Guide to Good Manners*. She lives in London.